AF408212

Jorgen Johansson

Hiking in Sweden

MOUNTAIN ROUTES AND GEAR

Author: Jorgen Johansson
Editor: Benny Eronson
Maps: Samuel Svärd
Photon: Jakob Sjölander: page 184; Tim Atterving: page 52. All other photos belong to the author
Layout: Informationsutvecklarna

Cover image from Alggajavrre, Sarek.

ISBN 978-91-979055-1-0

THANKS FROM THE AUTHOR

Many have contributed to this book, some with lots of information, some with small but important things. If I have forgotten someone I apologize. Without all the help I would have forgotten a lot more. First, I would like to thank Torkel och Annica Ideström for founding The Green Ribbon and unceasingly working to develop it. Others who have contributed with knowledge of routes, trails, and a lot of other things needed in a guidebook are Tim Atterving, Peter Bergström, Elaine Carlson, Eileen Coelus, Benny Eronson, Anna Gustafsson, Lina Hallebratt, Martin Nordesjö, Kim Norberg, Jonas Nordin, Karl-Johan Piehl, Erik Sandström, Ann Sjölander, Jakob Sjölander, Svante Sundelin, Karin Wahl and Helén Wollmén.

About the author

Jorgen Johansson is one of Sweden's most experienced wilderness hikers who has also hiked his version of The Green Ribbon. This and many other alternatives are something he shares in this book; routes along trails and off trail that are less known and lesser used. This means that even if you do not plan the thru-hike The Swedish Green Ribbon there are lots of tips and inspiration for shorter hikes all along the Swedish mountain range.

Jorgen is a well-known author with a number of books and articles on the outdoors, both in Swedish and English. In Swedish he is mostly known for the lightweight backpacker's bible *Vandra Fjäderlätt*, in English for the *Smarter Backpacking* series of books.

Content

Hiking the Swedish mountains – a walk on the wild side

This book will show how you can "walk on the wild side" through the Swedish mountains. This means exploring seldom visited places and having them all to yourself, be able to camp wherever you want and enjoy the challenge of picking the best trails or off-trail routes across wild country.

The framework for the route suggestions is something called The Swedish Green Ribbon. The Green Ribbon is a unique hiking trail because it is not a marked trail. It inspires you to walk 1300–1400 kilometers through the Swedish mountains. You pick existing trails or make short cuts between them in order to travel between Grövelsjön and Treriksröset (Three Country Cairn), where the borders of Sweden, Norway, and Finland meet.

Walking 1300 kilometers is not for everyone, so rest assured, the routes described can be used for a large number of shorter hikes.

A surprisingly large number of people who so far have hiked The Green Ribbon do it a lot on roads. Now asphalt has its advantages, but for walking with a pack, I find it boring, and hard on my feet. I will do my utmost in this book to suggest routes that will minimize walking on roads.

Still, it will not be possible to walk through the mountains without spending some distance on roads. You will walk in and out of trail-towns on roads, you will cross roads On occasion, and some vast waters are barring your way that can only be crossed on road bridges.

If you want to walk on roads or need to, because you are running out of time or food or care more about speed than mountains, they are always there for you on the maps. What I will do in this book is suggest the more beautiful routes, the ones that will give you a wilderness experience and (good) memories for life.

If you decide to follow me along The Green Ribbon I describe in this book, you will usually be given several options for different sections of your route. Some will suggest hiking on well-marked trails

0   100 km
Treriksröset
Abisko
Torneälven
Kalixälven
Bodø
Stora Lulevatten
Kvikkjokk
Luleälven
Hornavan
Hemavan
Storavan
Luleå
Storuman
Skellefteälven
NORWAY
Gäddede
SWEDEN
Skellefteå
Umeå
Östersund
Helags
Örnsköldsvik
Härnösand
Grövelsjön

At the start in Grövelsjön there is no doubt it is a long way to Treriksröset.

with an overnight hut approximately every 20 kilometers or so There will be stretches where you will not need a tent. But you cannot walk the entire Green Ribbon without sleeping in a tent on many nights. I prefer tenting because it gives me more freedom, brings me closer to nature, and lets me set my own pace on my walk. But at times, it is nice to get a roof over your head and a chance to get dry.

My ambition is to entice you away from the roads and the trails as much as possible, but it is always up to you. However, walking on the wild side demands some skills that you need to develop. The primary skill is route-finding or orienteering.

If you hike long, well-marked trails, you do not have to do much route-finding. Blazes and signs and a well-worn footpath will show you the way. For world-famous long-distance tracks like the Pacific Crest Trail, some apps will lead you by your hand from Mexico to Canada, providing you have a smartphone.

Walking on the wild side along with The Green Ribbon, you must be able to read a map, measure distances, and judge obstacles, like mountains, lakes, and creeks that must be managed along your route. All this boils down to judging the time it takes to cover different distances between places you must resupply. You do not want to run out of food, but neither do you want to carry more than you must.

Do not be daunted if you do not feel that you already have these skills. These days, route finding is much easier with GPS technology. You can go entirely by GPS, but I use it mostly to find exactly where I am at any given moment. With a GPS, it is very difficult to get lost. Paper maps are an essential backup and better for getting an overview than a small, or even a big, screen.

The Green Ribbon is the perfect hike to hone your cross-country competence. You have plenty of time and can almost always reconnect to well-maintained trails and seek shelter in overnight huts, should things get rough. You can start practicing this by leaving the trail for shorter periods and getting used to maps and GPS. Then you reconnect with the track. You can expand this to a 24-hour experience as your confidence and skills grow. If you are not comfortable doing this with your present skills, I recommend that you start your Green Ribbon hike from the south, at Grövelsjön. The distances between huts, trails, and people are more prominent than if you run into trouble in the desolate north.

So what is The Green Ribbon?

The Green Ribbon can also be the White Ribbon, should you endeavor to travel the mountains from end to end in winter. However, that is not something this book will cover.

The White and Green Ribbon is the brainchild of Swedish adventurers Annica and Torkel Ideström. As the official title is, the Scandinavian Mountaineers White and Green Ribbon were created during their "Around Sweden expedition" in 1997, when Annica and Torkel traveled under their own steam around their native country.

Their tour started on skis at Treriksröset. The couple skied south to the mountain lodge at Grövelsjön, usually considered the southernmost part of the Swedish mountain range. Annica and

Walking from Padjelanta National Park towards the peaks of Sarek National Park.

Torkel bicycled down to Svinesund, on the border between Norway and Sweden. At Svinesund, they switched to the Seapaddlers Blue Ribbon, kayaking around the entire Swedish coast, from Svinesund on the west coast, into the Baltic, and up to Haparanda on the Finnish border in the east. From Haparanda, they biked back to Treriksröset, completing the circle.

The Swedish Sea Paddler's Blue Ribbon has been a recognized challenge for many years, so it felt natural for Annica and Torkel to create something similar for the mountains, one challenge for winter and one for summer.

If you want to enter officially as a participant, register at www. vitagronabandet.se. This site is maintained by Torkel and Annica and is full of information, rules, inspiring photos, and a list of all who have completed The Green or The White Ribbon. On Facebook, there is also an official group where aspiring Ribboners can connect with others also planning a thru-hike or with those who have already done it and ask for advice about almost anything. If you search the internet, you will also find many blogs and videos to help you along.

The most remarkable thing about The Green Ribbon is that it is not a single trail, like European long-distance paths or American ones like the Appalachian Trail or the Pacific Crest Trail. Those trails are usually well marked and well-trodden, taking you through glorious areas. The spectacular landscape of the Alps or the Rockies with towering peaks and steep valleys has a downside, though. The topography with steep slopes, and often impenetrable brush in the valleys, forces you to use the artificial trails. There might also be right-of-way legalities stopping you from walking beside the path.

There is no single, marked trail in Sweden that leads from one end of the mountains to the other. There are many trails in most areas of our mountains, complete with overnight huts. But these trails are not always interconnected, and often there is no obvious trail or route that will lead to another well-marked trail with overnight huts, thus making the connection between the far north and the far south of our mountains. At the time of writing, there is an attempt to create a Swedish National Scenic Trail, called Via Suecia, from the southernmost part of Sweden at Smygehuk to Treriksröset. This trail exists on

Alggavagge, Sarek - a walk on the wild side.

maps and as a file for GPS devices, but it will probably be long before you find it marked in its entirety in the terrain.

However, the open tundra and the rolling hills (compared to the Alps or the Rocky Mountains) around the Arctic Circle in the Swedish mountains make it much easier to hike wherever you want. You are also free to walk wherever you want if it is not on the lot around somebody's house. Free to find your route and explore hidden valleys and unspoiled campsites far from crowds. Something you can do in very few parts of the world.

For the experienced and adventurous hiker, The Green Ribbon can genuinely be a walk on the wild side, where you can hike huge parts off-trail and stay away from overnight huts, relying on the shelter you carry.

For most hikers, the choice is probably not one or the other, only following trails or never following trails, of always staying in huts or never staying in huts. This book offers a smorgasbord, a buffet of different routes, and ways to hike The Green Ribbon. You pick what suits you from this array.

The many alternatives for picking a Green Ribbon hike of your design also make it more interesting to hike The Green Ribbon several times. There is no need to follow the same route everytime, but still chances to revisit your favorite mountain passes and campsites.

Or perhaps you do not want to hike the entire Green Ribbon in one continuous effort or even hike it at all. Then you can pick different sections from the book, a couple of days here, a week there, which might make you a Green Ribboner in two years or five or ten if that is your goal. Even if you are entirely uninterested in hiking the entirety of The Green Ribbon in one year or twenty years, this book will offer tons of inspiration about areas in the Swedish mountains you can explore. Places that in many cases have not been described in English before.

What this book is and is not

As mentioned, this book is a buffet, where you can pick what you want and skip what you do not. This works if you plan to hike the entire Green Ribbon in one long hike or if you're going to do The Green Ribbon piecemeal, a bit now and a bit then over several years. It also works if you plan to do some shorter hikes in the Swedish mountains and want some inspiration for a three-day or week-long hike. This book also works if you simply want something to dream about on dark December nights.

A smorgasbord, however big, is only a small selection of every dish that has ever seen the light of day. And, mathematically speaking, an infinite number of routes can be taken between points A and B on The Green Ribbon. In this case, between the endpoints Grövelsjön and Treriksröset.

If we stay with the mathematic parable, I assume if this infinite number of routes were to be described in a book, it would probably take an infinite number of trees left in this world to print it. Interestingly, this description of all possible routes between Grövelsjön and Treriksröset already exists. It is called a map. So, you do not need this book; all you need is to get the topographical maps covering the country between the endpoints of The Green Ribbon. Use the maps to plan your route, and off you go.

An exceptional and beautiful landscape; Klimpviken near Klimpfjäll.

This is what I have done myself for many years. But I have found that I save an awful lot of time by not having to invent every wheel, every route, myself. I find that I will get to the most beautiful places and have had a better experience when I return home from my vacation when I read up on other people's experiences.

This book will help you pick the cherries in the Swedish mountain range as you stroll along its spine. But it will not, because of the vast number of possible routes and routes described, be a description detailing every rock and log, every bridge or mountain or flower or hut. You need to get your maps. You cannot hike The Green Ribbon, or even parts of it, solely by the maps and descriptions in this book.

Hiking the tundra mountains of Sweden

Some basics

Here are some essential basics for those not used to hiking in the Scandinavian mountains (Norway, Sweden, and the northwestern-most part of Finland). You can breeze through this part if you are already an old mountain fox.

Thanks to the Gulf Stream going up the coast of Norway, the weather is much more benign in Scandinavia than in other areas of the world this close to the North Pole. But you will be traveling north of the Arctic Circle for much of The Green Ribbon. This means that temperatures can be low. In many areas, it rains a lot, and when it does, summertime temperatures are usually between 5–8 Celsius. In combination with wind, this means that hypothermia is always lurking. You must bring gear and have skills that will keep you as dry and warm as possible in these conditions—more on how to do this in the gear section.

Distances between people and houses in these mountains are longer than in most parts of Europe (except for Russia). Many Swedish trails are not heavily traveled, and in places, you can hike for several days without meeting anyone. This is doubly true if you travel cross country.

The advantages of this low population density are, in my opinion, so many that the disadvantages are outweighed. The main disadvantage is that you could be a long way from help if an accident should happen. On the other hand, do not be afraid of accidents. I have hiked for weeks on end during my entire adult life in the Swedish mountains and in even bigger wilderness areas in Alaska and Canada, without ever having an accident. Still, they happen, and in the gear section, I will advise on being prepared.

Sweden has an efficient mountain rescue organization that can be contacted through radiophones in many huts along the trails.

It is easy to leave the trail in the Swedish mountains and pick your own route.

Today you also have satellite transmitters that you can carry. You must bring the latter if you are an officially registered hiker on The Green Ribbon. On the other hand, cell phone coverage is not reliable all over when I am writing this. It certainly exists in many places, but you cannot rely on having it when you need it most.

All this said the mountains along The Green Ribbon have a good infrastructure. Along trails and even off-trail in many areas, you are seldom more than 10 kilometers, as the crow flies, from buildings and people. But 10 kilometers can of course sometimes be a lot if there are several peaks in the way.

There are overnight cabins along most trail systems, usually 20–25 kilometers apart. This is considered a distance most people will be able to hike in a day. You can walk from cabin to cabin in areas like

On the horizon Fältjägarstugan, a hut managed på STF.

that, sleep inside, dry out your gear, and have a lovely evening with other hikers. The kitchen will be self-service, only in bigger lodges, usually at road heads, will the staff serve meals.

The huts are usually owned and managed either by the STF, the Swedish Tourist Association, or publicly owned. The regional authorities, Länstyrelsen, do generally manage the publicly-owned huts. The Sami manage some huts, usually in a cooperative organization.

You will pay an overnight fee if you sleep inside or a day fee if you camp near the cabin and use facilities like the privy, kitchen, or drying gear. There is usually a host in the cabin for the STF huts and the Sami-managed huts whom you can pay. Many publicly-owned, regionally operated (often seldom visited) overnight huts depend on you being honest and paying afterward to a bank account usually posted in the huts or on the internet. Cash usually works, but other forms of payment are getting more and more common. They typically depend on if the area has mobile phone coverage.

Rest huts have simple furnish – and are not always newly built.

The above holds for the Swedish mountains, should you choose to walk part of The Green Ribbon in Norway, I find the cabins being cozier and better kept. You must usually book ahead and sometimes collect a key (occasionally valid for Sweden also). The huts in Norway are typically owned and managed by the Norwegian Tourist Association (DNT). Their website has more information on this. My knowledge is limited; I have always stayed in my tent while hiking the Norwegian parts of The Green Ribbon.

Along the more frequented trails, you will also find rest huts. These are usually located about halfway between the overnight huts. So, you will be able to find shelter, a roof over your head, at approximately every 10 kilometers along trails like Kungsleden and many other well-traveled trails.

These rest huts are good places to stop for lunch and coffee in wet and windy conditions. The rest huts are small and usually contain a couple of wooden bunks, a table, and a wood stove. They are not meant for overnight use but are emergency shelters, particularly from winter snowstorms. There is seldom firewood available in summer; it is usually shipped to the huts when winter comes. Do not use any firewood unless you are indeed in an emergency.

In some villages and towns, you might find campgrounds, hostels, or hotels owned and managed by locals. In some villages and most towns, you will also find a store where you can buy food and fuel (alcohol is generally available, gas canisters not always so during my thru-hike). Some of these local businesses will accept, usually for a fee or the agreement that they get your business, that you send a box ahead to be collected as you pass through on your hike. That way, you can send food and gear to be picked up by yourself. Since post offices are scarce, do not expect to send "drift boxes" from town to town, like you can on many American trails. However, many village stores also run a postal service, so you have to check whether it is possible before your hike.

Since these businesses, campgrounds, hostels, and stores tend to come and go, it is useless, or at least very time-sensitive, to mention most of them in a book like this. A book might last twenty years; a business might be gone tomorrow. Or go to a new owner, website, or phone number.

The tundra can be steep, like here, near Kebnekaise.

The tundra can also be as flat, as here near Treriksröset.

My advice is to search the internet for what is available in places you know you will pass on your hike. Many of them will have web pages. Using phone numbers and e-mail addresses provided, you can contact them and make arrangements. Almost all enterprises in villages and towns you encounter will take credit cards. The exception is often people supplying boat transport across lakes and some overnight huts without landlines or cell phone coverage. So, I always try to guesstimate and bring cash in local currency.

Hiking tundra

Hiking The Green Ribbon means walking a lot of tundras. You will also encounter sub-alpine forests with birch, spruce, and pine close to the tundra. In most parts of the world, the timber lines are made up of evergreen forests; in Scandinavia, it is birch.

When talking about the tundra, I refer almost entirely to what is technically "alpine tundra." This is defined as an area that does not contain trees because of high elevation or a latitude near the poles. It seamlessly merges with "arctic/polar tundra" defined by permafrost, where the subsoil is frozen year-round. Arctic tundra only exists in the northernmost areas of the Swedish mountains, close to Treriksröset. I cannot seriously say that I notice much difference between these tundra types when hiking, but I am no expert.

The main thing about tundra is that it lacks trees, and an old Swedish proverb says: "The forest is the poor man's coat". This means roughly that the forest will give a certain amount of protection from wind and rain and provide fuel for fires. The opposite is true of the tundra, and in high winds, nothing beats getting down into the forest, especially if the wind is mixed with rain. Building fires on the tundra is tricky, although skilled people, mostly reindeer herders and hunters, manage. I recommend that you avoid any fire on the tundra unless in an emergency, plant growth is extremely slow, and many people building fires will seriously deplete the vegetation.

At high elevations in all parts of the world, you will sooner or later reach the tree line and then the tundra. In more southerly locations of our globe, like the Alps and the Rocky Mountains, the tundra is usually limited to high mountains and high passes. The tree line in these areas is not many kilometers away most of the time. And below the tree line, you will find some, and sometimes almost total, protection from wind and rain. This is an essential difference since the tundra of the Swedish mountains can and will stretch for tens of kilometers and lots more in the far north. So, you cannot count on being able to retreat into the forest if a rainstorm hits. You need gear and skills to manage—more on how to do this in the gear section.

In my experience, hiking the Scandinavian mountains is equal to walking the northernmost parts of Alaska, which is to say that it is among the most demanding hiking, weather-wise, in the world. It is far from the High Sierra of California, where the sun shines continuously for weeks on end, and a sudden squall will be over in hours.

Do not let this frighten you; it can be managed, but you should be aware of the differences, especially if you have only hiked in other areas than Scandinavia.

Hiking off-trail

Maybe I had better repeat that hiking off-trail in the tundra mountains of Sweden is more straightforward than doing it in mountainous areas in many other places. It is not something to be afraid of,

When you leave Sarek through the valley of Basstavagge, Lake Sitojaure is waiting for you.

and I prefer it in many ways. Following a well-marked trail can be pretty dull. You do not have to use much of your brain, like driving a car down an empty highway. In this book, I will try to tell you about the joys you can experience when you travel by your wits and skills. This does not mean that traveling off-trail is easy, but few rewarding things in life are easy. What you get out of something usually stands in relation to your investment. Neither does it mean that it cannot be learned. For many, it is primarily a mental thing.

Hiking many of the trails along The Green Ribbon, you will find them well marked with red/orange paint on trees and rocks or cairns. There are usually bridges across major creeks and board-walks across marshlands. However, some trails are poorly maintained, the markings are gone or invisible, the path is periodically overgrown with plants. This is where a GPS is your best friend.

The trails will furnish you with many things that you must manage by yourself when you hike cross country. One important thing

This kind of terrain is not nice to hike in. Avoid if you can (Salmmecahca).

you have to address when going off-trail is direction. You have to make sure that you go where you plan to go and end up where you want to be. Map, compass, and GPS will help you with this.

A GPS device might break down or run out of battery power. A paper map and a compass are essential and valuable backups. They do not weigh much, and they never fail. But these days, I find I use the GPS in my smartphone, complete with a map, for 90 percent of all route-finding. Especially on trails. This will probably only increase in the future.

The huge advantage is that the GPS always shows you where you are. This way, you do not have to painstakingly count your steps in dead reckoning between waypoints or otherwise keep track of every turn. This suits a lazy person like me perfectly.

You need to have basic skills in reading a map. This means knowing how to identify (too) steep terrain, narrow gorges, rivers, and other obstacles you should avoid or will have to manage. You need this skill to plan where to pick your way to reach your goal. The

GPS and compass are tools to make sure you are interpreting your plotted route from the map into the real world.

Picking a route on the tundra is easy compared to route-finding in the forest. In decent weather, you can often see for long distances on the tundra. Mountains can be identified from the map. The pass or valley you aim for can be seen for miles away. You can fairly easily pick your way across the terrain, looking ahead, avoiding things that might slow you down or even stop you.

Hiking across open areas like that, I find myself thinking in what you might call three dimensions: Long-distance, middle distance, and short distance.

Number one is the long-distance goal, perhaps the valley between the two peaks on the horizon. The second is the middle distance; should I go left or right of the little lake several hundred meters or even a kilometer away. Finally, the short distance is perhaps the next 0-10 meters: Should I go left or right of the little bush, what are the consequences of this for how I will negotiate the rocks further ahead, all the way down to where to put my foot down next.

Another benefit that a trail brings is to ease your passage, and I do not mean direction finding, but effortwise. This is especially true of old paths that have been laid out by people living and moving about in the mountains, often carrying heavy burdens. It is a joy to follow trails like those because they sort of flow through the woods, across the tundra, taking the way of least resistance. They bring you uphill and downhill in the most energy-conserving way that is possible, given the terrain.

It is all about managing gravity, which is worth a chapter of its own.

Managing gravity

Finding your way cross country means that gravity must be managed. Its effects must be minimized. This to conserve your energy and protect the bones, ligaments, and muscles that will take you to your goal in good shape, without injuries, and in good cheer.

As far as energy consumption goes there is, within limits, not much difference between carrying a heavy pack on flat ground and carrying a light pack on flat ground. But as soon as the ground tilts just a bit, heading uphill, you pay a price for your heavy load. You will immediately notice that your breath is coming quicker and that it is just plain hard work going uphill, especially if it is steep.

Going downhill might be nice if you are on a bike and can coast along, not so if you are walking, because gravity is eating away at your body again. To make a controlled descent, you must use the same muscles, ligaments, and bones as for an ascent. So going downhill is also harder than walking on the flat, albeit not as hard as going uphill. It is a lot harder if you have to control a heavy pack in addition to your body weight. By this you, hopefully learn that you should avoid your pack being heavier than necessary. More on that in the gear chapter.

What I am driving at is that to minimize the effects of gravity on your well-being, you have to avoid going uphill or downhill as much as possible.

Hey, you say, we are in the mountains; they are made of uphills and downhills. We cannot avoid going uphill or downhill. That is why we are hiking here. Otherwise, we would be sitting in a sidewalk café in Rome.

True. Please note the words "as much as possible". This is what managing gravity is about. You cannot beat gravity; it eventually wins. In the end, it will put us all six feet under. But to postpone this, we must strive to be a bit smart. So, if you cannot avoid going uphill, do it where the slope is less steep. Do not walk up, over a slight hill, or even a bump in the ground, and then down on the other side. Walk around it. Do not walk down into a hollow, or even a slight depression in the ground, and then up on the other side. Walk around it. Minimize your ups and downs.

It all sounds easy but becomes complicated by reality. If it is a low hillock but a long way around, maybe it is less energy-consuming to walk up and over it. Sure, we all must make decisions and we will all make mistakes, but my tip is that going around is almost always less energy-consuming than going up and over. As you learn by the gravity (pun intended) of your mistakes, your exceptions from this rule will become more and more correct.

Sometimes you will make the wrong decision, but it all adds up on a long hike or even on a long day. Keep this thing about minimi-

Hiking in the Swedish mountains, you cannot avoid wetlands.

zing the effects of gravity in mind. You will come out a winner, less fatigued and less prone to stumble and injure yourself or make stupid decisions in tricky situations.

Hiking the wetlands

I will repeat this many times in this book; the Swedish mountains are wet. Lots of precipitation and thin topsoil mean that you in flat areas you will have to hike a lot of wetlands.

Wetlands come in different shapes so some definitions might be helpful. Bogs are generally areas that have been lakes once upon a time. Some are drier, and some are wetter. It also depends on the weather or if it is early or late in the season. Quaking bogs are one variety that resembles walking on a waterbed. This is due to a more or less thick layer of vegetation that is sort of floating on top of a more saturated layer. Bogs are usually walkable.

Marshland and bogs are usually easy to hike.

Marshland is usually found near lakes, rivers, and riverbanks; it is often, but not always, flooded and covered with a grass-like growth. It usually is walkable.

Swamps are areas that are always wet, usually very wet. They are seldom walkable, or perhaps I should say they are walkable in patches.

Very often, you find these wetlands mixed, particularly bogs and swamps. Many wet areas on well-maintained trails will have longer or shorter stretches of boardwalks to carry you across. This is done both to protect the fragile vegetation that will otherwise quickly turn to mud and help you as a hiker.

Not all trails and not all wet areas along the trail will have boardwalks. So, it will be almost impossible to hike The Green Ribbon without getting your feet wet. I am somewhat amused when I hear of how much time and energy some hikers spend trying to avoid getting their feet wet. And how frustrated they become when they fail.

I would not want every damp spot from Grövelsjön to Treriksröset covered with planks. In my opinion, it is better to accept that you will get wet and chose footwear that can handle this. This is covered in another chapter.

Where there is a trail and no planks, the bog, as mentioned, often tends to become churned into mud. This is usually more due to people driving quad bikes than hikers' feet, but the latter certainly also can create mud. Quads have increased as means of transporting and transportation for local people in the mountains in the last ten years. Even in the most protected areas, the national parks, they are allowed to be used by Sami reindeer herders.

I find it very difficult to demand that local people trying to make a living in the areas I am hiking through, for my pleasure, should not be allowed to use modern technology. But the quads certainly make a mess, and I was a lot happier 30 years ago when they did not exist. Quad traffic will probably increase even more, and it will not go away. What should and could be done about it is not in the scope of this book. As a hiker, I must manage the situation. All you can do is, whenever possible, to avoid wet, black mud that has been churned into a mess.

My rule number one when walking bogs is to put my feet where there is vegetation. These areas can differ a bit. Bogs differ, some areas are dry and solid, and you will find no doubt in your mind whether they will carry your weight or not. Some areas are wet. Very wet. They are, in fact, a gathering of ponds with swamps in between.

My rule of thumb for hiking bogs and swamps is that stepping on green is okay, stepping on brown usually is fine and stepping on black is like trying to walk on water, a no-no. I will sink.

The quaking bogs mentioned above are swamps/ponds covered by a more or less solid network of plants and roots. When you walk on these areas, you will feel that you are on something elastic, that something sort of wobbles under your feet. This is quite all right in most cases, but you should avoid walking on quaking bogs. Retreat calmly and look for a way around.

If a short stretch of quaking bog is unavoidable, remember it is a bit like riding a bicycle. Remain calmly in motion. If you stop, your weight might after a while break through the organic webbing supporting you, and you will sink to your knees or your groin.

Do not get terrified should this occur; you will not be swallowed up and sink into oblivion. You might sink to your knees or groin, but your pack will keep you floating. It is usually less of a problem than falling into water, provided you can swim. Just work your way back to where you came from and get up. I have walked a lot of bogs and have never had an accident like the above. I have been down to below my knees and then retreated.

In my experience, it is fairly obvious where to step and where not to when walking the wetlands. You learn quickly. There is usually a way around boggy areas, but bogs are often easy to walk on when traveling cross country, particularly in forested areas. They are flat, with no rocks, trees, or brush (except around the fringes) to battle. When traveling off-trail I often look for bogs and then make my way across.

Just do not expect to keep your feet dry unless you use knee-high rubber boots. And not always with those.

Crossing water
LOW RISK CROSSINGS

Even if you follow the most beaten paths through the mountains, there will not be a bridge over every stream you encounter. Early in the season, during snow-melt, you will have to ford plenty of these streams every day; late in the season, they will be fewer.

Most fords will be through shallow, slow-moving water, not demanding or dangerous unless you make simple mistakes.

One fundamental mistake can sometimes be to balance on rocks sticking out of the water to keep your feet dry. If a slippery rock dumps you and your pack on other rocks in the stream, you can hurt yourself. I am not saying I never step on rocks across creeks, but I am careful, have poles for support, and only do it across small creeks with little or slow-moving water.

Another risky business is wading in your bare feet, particularly if you hold your shoes in one hand. You can slip, fall and lose one or more shoes, as well as hurt yourself. You might also cut your feet on sharp, underwater rocks or have a rock roll over your foot, damaging

Wearing mesh shoes, you do not have to stop and change footwear for a ford; you just keep walking.

it. Even a minor injury to a foot might be a serious thing in the mountains and can put an end to your hike.

The root of the problems described above is usually the fear of getting your feet wet. So, we are back to the discussion on hiking wetlands, and to footwear, which has a separate chapter, but a few words are needed in this context as well.

I hike in mesh shoes that are almost constantly damp and I do not worry about getting my feet wet. Combined with thin synthetic runners' pants this makes fording small creeks very simple. I just walk into the water without missing a stride, using my beloved hiking poles for support, exit the creek on the other side, and keep on walking. After five minutes, my trousers are almost dry, except perhaps for an inch at the bottom, and my feet have gone from soaked, back to their regular dampness.

When traveling solo through the Brooks Range of Alaska for a month, I forded shallow creeks and rivers between 30–50 times per day. Sometimes I walked for hundreds of meters in the water because it was easier than walking on the banks. In my opinion, mesh shoes are the most practical footwear for really wet country.

If you are using regular hiking boots and judge that there is a risk of water running over the top of these, you have two choices when coming to a creek.

One is to take your boots off, strapping them to the pack, and then use a pair of lightweight shoes brought for wading and camp use. If you do not have shoes like that, the least you should do is to wear your thickest socks to protect your feet from hurt and cuts.

The second method is to pull on your rain pants and make a waterproof connection with your boots by tying these pants, with strings or straps, around your ankles. This, of course, means that your boots really have to be waterproof. Many boots are waterproof in the store, the question is always for how long.

Both these methods work, but are a hassle, especially if you, after switching back into your ordinary hiking outfit, discover another creek that needs the same process after a couple of hundred meters. And after that yet another... This is when you might start taking risks out of impatience, such as balancing on rocks across the stream, even if they look chancy and slippery and a fall could hurt you a lot.

HIGH-RISK CROSSINGS

So far, we have only covered the low-risk, easy fords. You will also run into significant creeks that are deep, wide, and with rapidly moving water. These can be dangerous. Even experienced people, like Sami reindeer herders, have drowned during fords.

A rule of thumb says that if the water moves very fast, you should not ford if the water is over your knees. Water current is very powerful, and the depth in midstream is not easy to judge from the banks and might differ quite a bit from where you are entering the creek.

Sometimes you cannot avoid deep water, though. You must consider how fast it is moving and act accordingly. If I follow a trail and come to such a creek, the best place to ford is usually somewhere close to where the trail meets the creek. That is usually why the trail is located there in the first place. I look for the broadest part of the creek in that area, because it is where the water is less deep and will run at the lowest speed. Simple physics.

Ideally, this wide spot is halfway between a couple of bends in the creek. This means the deepest part of the creek is more or less in the middle. If I try to ford at a bend, I will find the deepest part is where I am getting in or on the opposite side. This depends on whether I am inside or outside the bend. Water rushes into the bend and hits the opposing, outside bank; it runs faster and digs deeper into the creek bottom and bank there, than inside the bend. Simple physics.

From where I am standing, I check the opposite bank for a place to exit the water. Is it in a bend with a steep bank and water that might be waist-deep even if it is knee-deep where I stand? Then I might not be able to climb out of the creek, especially if shrubs are leaning over the water from the bank.

After finding an optimal spot I pick a route across the stream as ideal from all these aspects as possible and begin to ford. I love my hiking poles and would never ford without at least one pole to hold on to in fast-moving water. Bent forward in a wide stance, with my poles and legs as corners of a structure, I face slightly upstream and start to move, one pole or one foot at a time. Three of my four supports are always firmly anchored. If the water is swift-moving and deep, I might face almost entirely upstream to resist the powerful force of the water better and then move sideways like a crab.

This is how I inch my way across a difficult ford. When getting close to the other side, I resist the urge to take a few quick steps "to get it over with." Instead, I repeat the mantra: "It ain't over 'til it's over."

You will probably not encounter many fords like this on well-traveled trails, but early in the season, it can happen. These crossings are more likely to occur if you walk on the wild side. So let us stay there for a while.

There are also deep, slow-moving, narrow creeks you sometimes run into while crossing bogs, not seldom close to lakes. These creeks have dug down through the soft organic material of the bog until

A ford of medium difficulty.

they have hit rock bottom, or more often gravel. These creeks might be no more than two or three meters wide but two meters deep and just as deep in all directions, without any shallows, as they meander across the bog.

The pack will make you buoyant if you get in above your waist in waters like that with your backpack on. This is because the pack contains a lot of air, usually enclosed in waterproof bags and food packages. I have balanced and trod water for a meter or so until my feet have hit bottom on the other side. This is not pleasant; it feels tippy. I am out of control and might roll over, but the slow-moving water means that I probably do not run any significant risk of drowning. Still, not a nice feeling, so the best bet for these narrow but deep channels is to take your pack off and walk/swim with it ahead of you.

This brings us to the technique I use if I want to, or need to, cross a major, deep creek or small river with slow-moving, not rapidly rushing, water. Waterways like that I find less risky to cross if I make a controlled swim instead of attempting an uncontrolled ford. I learned the technique in the Swedish Army. This is something you should try at home, on a beach on a warm and sunny day perhaps, before launching into it on a rainy day by a mountain river, with low blood sugar and a bus you must catch, somewhere down the trail.

Doing a stream crossing like this can be potentially dangerous; I hardly ever use it. There are usually bridges somewhere across major waterways.

I consider several things before deciding to swim or not. The water in a mountain river will be cold, even in summer. Most likely 10–15 C. In water that cold, I can get hypothermic fast. Using the rain gear instead of swimming naked works a bit like a poor man's wet suit; it reduces loss of body heat from water washing over my skin quite a bit. Also, I am not without clothes, and my feet have shoes on, should the worst happen, which would be losing my pack with all my gear, watching it take off downstream.

A swim like this is probably a no-go if I think I will spend more than five-ten minutes in the water. It depends on the water temperature, of course. So, the width of the crossing is essential and must be judged.

I also consider how swift the current is. This is difficult in rivers; I find it easy to underestimate. One way of getting an impression of the current speed is to throw a stick into the water as far as I can. I then watch how slowly or swiftly the stick moves downstream. Then I look at the opposite bank and downstream. I am probably standing at a spot where I can easily get into the water, and the bank straight across should look similar. But there is a risk that the current will carry me downstream, away from the bank straight across. So, I check that bank a bit downstream, to see that it does not become very steep or covered with brush and trees, where I might become entangled and unable to get out of the water.

If it feels doable, I strip completely, always fun if the mosquitoes are in season, and put on my rain jacket, rain pants, and shoes. My other clothing goes into a waterproof bag, with electronics like GPS/phone/camera, in my backpack. I wrap my tent around the outside of the pack to keep it a little drier. I try to tie it into a nice package, using the tent guy lines.

These narrow but deep creeks across bogs can be tricky to cross. This is near the Lainio River in the far north.

I carry this package in my arms into the water; it will float nice and high because of all the air inside. I keep walking into the water, pushing the floating pack in front of me until my feet lose contact with the river bottom. Then I start swimming with my feet, holding the pack in front of me as a floating device. The current must be managed. As describe in the later section about packrafts, when ferrying across a stream I must aim roughly at 45 degrees upstream and swim/paddle in that direction, to compensate for the current. The current will pull me downstream if I try to swim straight across.

I keep this up until I feel the bottom, near the opposite riverbank. I then walk out of the water with my pack, unwrap it, and put on my dry clothes.

Crossing waterways can be dangerous, and I am describing this swimming technique with a certain trepidation; some people will probably accuse me of recommending a hazardous activity. But I do it because I feel it is less dangerous than trying to ford a fast-moving stream, especially if you are not an experienced wader. The risk for injury, in my opinion, is bigger if you fall, fully clothed, with a pack on, and are swept downstream, perhaps towards rocks or rapids.

One last tip. Even a major, fast-moving creek or river will slow down when it enters a lake. This means that the silt carried by the stream will sink to the bottom when the current dies down. Often this silt is deposited in a sort of a semi-circle around the mouth of the river. Hundreds of years of silt sinking this way mean that it is not uncommon to have shallows of silt that you might walk on in places like this. A sort of curved ford across the mouth of the river, a bit into the lake, with water sometimes not more than knee-deep, even if the river mouth and the lake on both sides are a lot deeper. It might be worth it to spend some time looking for a place like that. You will not always find it, but perhaps more often than one would think. So, it pays to remember that the shallowest place in a river might be right where it enters a lake.

This section is not a comprehensive guide to fording, just a few tricks, and tips. I do not know everything. I have, for instance, never forded in a group where the members support each other going across a stream. Fording is like bicycling; you cannot learn it by reading a book. You must practice. But a book can make your learning curve a lot shorter. There are courses that teach fording techniques. Take care; crossing streams can be hazardous but usually is easy. Do not let worries about crossing creeks scare you away from walking some wild country.

Drinking water

By now, you are getting fed up with me talking about how wet the mountains can be. One upside is that there is plenty of drinking water almost everywhere.

Since water is heavy, this means it is hardly ever necessary to carry water. Within the next five minutes, or thirty minutes, you will usually have passed one or many small streams. It all depends on terrain and season, of course. Still, many hikers seem unable not to

Here you can just dip your cup and drink straight from The Earth Mother.

have water bottles riding on their shoulder straps. Something that might be necessary in drier, or more polluted, parts of the world like the High Sierras or the Alps. Still, water might be scarce at higher elevations after snowmelt and with no glaciers around. However, areas like that are usually too high up for people hiking The Green Ribbon.

When I say drinking water, I mean just that. I have hiked the Swedish mountains for decades and never purified any water. I love just being able to dip my cup in a trickle, stream, or lake and drink straight from the breast of Mother Nature. And I have never been sick to my stomach because of this.

A critical rule for judging water quality is to study its source, where it comes from. Are there people, buildings, villages, or livestock, like cows and sheep, upstream? Usually, you can determine this from the map. Reindeer do not count as livestock; from this aspect, they can be considered wildlife, like moose and deer.

I do not drink from water that seems suspect. However, what I consider suspect is not water with a brownish tinge and a taste that differs a bit from the chlorinated stuff coming out of my tap at home. A brownish tinge is only natural and 999 times out of 1000 completely safe. Water that has a smell is not necessarily bad, but the water that smells bad usually is. Trust your senses.

I always use the smallest water source available because there is less risk that it comes from a contaminated source. However, the reverse logic might also work; a huge amount of water will dilute possible pollutants. Lakes, big and small, with no habitation around, are low risk.

I also prefer water that moves, not standing still, being stagnant. However, I have drunk my share from strange-looking puddles in bogs without getting sick.

The majority of small or big streams you are likely to encounter along The Green Ribbon do not come from any habitation. And even so, today, all houses, villages, and towns are required to manage and purify their water before it is let out into nature. So have no fear as far as potable water goes; in the mountains between Grövelsjön and Treriksröset, you can live like in a true wilderness.

Wildlife

The most common mammal you will encounter on The Green Ribbon trails is probably reindeer. Unless perhaps it happens to be a rodent year. Rodent years are infrequent these days; consider yourself lucky if you hit one. The rule of thumb half a lifetime ago used to be that every 4th year or so was a rodent year. Not so for a long time. If there is one, you might see many of the famous lemmings, some who seem to fear nothing, at least not hikers.

Reindeer are semi-domestic animals, meaning they are all owned by somebody and occasionally gathered, driven, marked, and slaughtered. You could say that they are semi-used to people. They will keep their distance but will not scramble away and hide once they have identified you as a human being. All truly wild animals will try to get out of your way long before you discover their existence. All other occurrences are just coincidental.

I have hiked extensively in the Swedish mountains for many decades and have yet to encounter any of the four big predators: wolf, bear, lynx, and wolverine. For comparison, hiking in North America, I have seen many black bears and grizzlies, while simply walking along.

The Green Ribbon moves almost exclusively through reindeer country, and the Sami do not accept wolves there, so you will have no chance of encountering any wolves.

If you do not take great pains to do so, the likelihood that you will see any big predator is minimal. The possibility that they will in any way harm you is nil. It has never happened. A few instances of bears attacking hunters have occurred because they have brought loose dogs or shot and injured the bear.

If you hike with a dog, you must always keep it on a leash. Not only for your own sake or the dog's protection but because it is the law for the entire country all summer, usually until August 20th. In many national parks, like Sarek, you are not allowed to bring a dog, even leashed, unless you are a reindeer herder.

As long as you are hiking along, trying to make mileage, you will only chance upon the odd moose, roe deer, red fox, or arctic fox. To watch wildlife, you have to pick places where they are likely to move, especially at dawn or dusk, and sit very still and quiet for a long time at a suitable vantage point. Binoculars are very helpful.

What you will see and hear plenty of is birds. Suppose you hike the entire Green Ribbon during one season. In that case, you will walk through their whole cycle of summer life, which is a beautiful experience—beginning with the myriads of ways to attract a mate with colors, sounds, and movement, through the frenzied feeding of the voracious small ones later on, to some parents taking off with the new generation, flying south as winter looms.

Many of these birds have traveled far to get to the Swedish mountains; some come even from Antarctica. The reason for these journeys is the abundance of light beneath the Midnight Sun, leading to an explosion of life to feed on for a brief month or two. One of these explosions important for many birds is the one of insects.

As hikers, we are primarily concerned with insects like mosquitoes and biting flies, some of diminutive size. Insects can be a

The reindeer gather on the cool snow on a hot summer's day.

problem, and very much so if you are allergic. When you curse them, remember that they are an essential part of the food chain, even if it at that time is is apparent that it is you who is part of their food chain.

Thin microfiber clothing, bug repellent, and a head net are useful for keeping you sane while on the trail, especially during breaks. You also need to protect yourself from insects at night, with a suitably equipped shelter.

Ticks and similar creatures have difficulty surviving the harsh winters up north, so you do not have to worry about them.

Gear for the Swedish mountains

The philosophy and physiology of weight

The weight of your gear is more important when it comes to long-distance hiking than shorter hikes. For a quick overnight trip, perhaps just a few kilometers from a car, most people can carry all they want, including fresh food and a bag-in-box of wine. But if you will be hiking for weeks or months, you should be carrying as little as possible. My rule for many years has been, not to use the lightest gear available but to use to use the lightest gear that does the job.

What is needed to do the job depends on where and when you are hiking. As I have already pointed out, in my opinion, the Scandinavian mountains are among the most demanding areas to hike in the world. This is because of comparatively low temperatures, lots of precipitation, and often very little natural protection from high winds.

Low pack weight is especially important if you are not a young and strong person. I and thousands of others have been using lightweight gear for decades in the most demanding circumstances and found them safe, comfortable, and a lot more painless to carry for weeks on end. In fact, for a long-distance hike, I would say that a light pack diminishes the risk for stress injuries and falling on steep or uneven surfaces. Also, if you sprain an ankle and need to hobble to the nearest road, it is easier to do with 10 kilos on your back than with 20 kilos on your back. The same goes if you, for some reason, have to carry your hiking partner's backpack.

Remember that Mother Earth and gravity are not affected by marketing messages saying that a particular product, despite its weight, is so marvelously and innovatively engineered that it practically transports itself. Nothing on your hike will move you, nor the things you carry, from A to B except your very own muscles, ligaments, and bones. And the less extra weight those muscles, ligaments, and bones have to handle, the less strain it will put on your body.

Let's face it, after carrying 10 kilos for five hours; you will feel more comfortable and happier than after taking 20 kilos. After five or fifteen days with a heavy load, your body might quit on you. Or

Even a large pack can be light. This 70-liter bag only weighs 1 kilo.

at least complain bitterly. Joints might be aching. Blisters will burn your feet. Maybe an ankle got twisted from overexertion. You take painkillers to struggle on.

It is your choice. Let me repeat; I use the lightest gear that does the job. Fortunately, thanks to new, robust materials, plenty of lightweight gear today does the job.

Practical advice on weight and gear

Let us get down to some advice that is more hands-on. I am a lightweight backpacker, but not an ultralight one. My pack base weight, the things I always carry except food and fuel, is usually around 6,5–7 kilos for shorter or longer hikes in the Swedish mountains. For three-season backpacking, this works very well for me. I have used the same kind of gear for 15 years, not only in Scandinavia but also in the Brooks Range of Alaska and northern Canada. I can honestly say that it works even in rough conditions.

Many people hike in the Swedish mountains with lower base weights than mine. Still, the overwhelming majority of backpackers I meet have huge packs and heavy loads, in my opinion, completely unnecessarily.

I have written several books in both Swedish and English about lightweight backpacking, so I will be brief and focus only on what I think is a top priority, gear-wise, for someone hiking the Swedish mountains.

The essential trick to lighten your load is to look at "the three big ones" and how much they weigh. The three big ones are your backpack, sleep system, and shelter. The pack is almost always the heaviest piece of equipment for hikers, even lightweight hikers. The sleep system consists of a sleeping bag/quilt and sleeping pad; the shelter is your tent.

So, forget about titanium cook pots versus aluminium ones and shortening the handle of your toothbrush until you have made sure of "three for three."

"Three for three" or "343" if you want to be cute, is a way of describing something I first wrote about in my book Smarter Backpacking more than ten years ago. It means that your three big ones should not collectively weigh more than three kilos.

Considering there are lots of backpacks on the market that, by themselves empty, weigh three kilos or more, this might seem a ridiculous recommendation. Rest easy; it is a piece of cake to achieve.

For starters, only because The Green Ribbon is a long hike it does not mean you need a huge pack for that reason. You are not hiking 1300 kilometers in one go. It is divided into a long chain with links of 3–7-day hikes, depending on how you organize it.

You hardly ever need to carry food for more than one week between resupply points. So, in my opinion, a backpack with a volume of 50-60 litres is big enough. There are plenty of packs this size today that weighs only one kilo or slightly more.

Some packs weigh 1,5 kilos, with a volume of 90–100 litres that can stand up to loads of 50 kilos if you can stand up to that. I know I cannot. There is no NEED for us, ordinary mortals, to ever use a pack that weighs more than 1,5 kilos. If you do, it is simply a matter

A lightweight sleeping bag weighing 600 grams. Good for -1C.

of choice. And since you must carry it yourself, no skin off my nose. I am just trying to help.

Regarding the sleep system my advice is for you to pick a sleeping bag or quilt rated for 0 degrees Celsius. It will be enough most of the time unless you travel very early or very late in the season. If you get cold in it, put on all your clothes, including rain gear (as long as it is dry). If this does not help, my favourite trick is to put a bottle of hot water inside the bag.

High-quality down sleeping bags rated for 0 C will weigh around 500–700 grams. They are usually expensive but will last 10–15 years with undiminished insulating capacity, even if you use them a lot. Some people do not want to use a down bag (or quilt). In that case, you should be aware that a comparable synthetic sleeping bag probably will be almost twice as heavy and will lose quite a bit of its insulative properties during a long walk for a month or more, like The Green Ribbon. This is because synthetics do not bounce back to their original volume as well as down does after being repeatedly compressed in your pack.

Underneath your sleeping bag, I recommend an inflatable mattress weighing less than 500 grams for comfort as well as insulation. It need not be full length, if hips and shoulders rest softly. Be careful; there are many mattresses like that weighing more than one kilo. I also always bring a full-length cell foam pad that I use for sitting/laying on during breaks and underneath the inflatable mattress at night. The foam pad is also very useful should the inflatable pad spring a leak that cannot be found and fixed on the trail. This has happened to me several times. 150–200 grams for the cell pad is attainable.

I will dedicate a separate section to shelters, but plenty of tents on the market will do the job on The Green Ribbon and weigh less than one kilo if you hike solo. If you are two people walking together, there are plenty of tents weighing less than two kilos. Calculating 3 for 3 depends on dividing the weight of the tent you share with a partner. It does not mean that you should split the tent between you while hiking. Should you lose contact for some reason, it is better that one of you should have a functioning tent than none of you.

So, summing it up, you can hike the Swedish mountains in complete safety and comfort with a backpack at one kilo, a sleeping bag and pads at one kilo, and a tent also weighing one kilo (per person). Voila, three kilos for the three big ones. Or 343, three for three...

When I hiked The Green Ribbon, my three big ones weighed 2,2 kilos for the first half and 3,0 for the second, northern part of the walk, where I beefed up with a warmer sleeping bag and a sturdier tent.

Shelters for The Green Ribbon

Since first discovering American ultralight backpacking, I have spent about 20 years testing and using a wide variety of gear and techniques that can be found under that label. I have done so in Scandinavia, continental USA, Alaska, Canada, and Australia. This does not mean that I am always right, but it is from this background I want to share some findings. In the Scandinavian mountains, you usually need more clothing than in many places while hiking, something I will get back to, but the most significant difference I have found is shelters.

A tarp with a bug- and windproof nest is my favorite for forest hiking.

Many ultralight and sub-ultralight gear work best in more benign climates than the Swedish mountains, usually with warmer temperatures and less precipitation. Most hiking in the USA, where ultralight techniques were developed, takes place below the tree line or with the tree line reasonably close. If the shit hits the fan in these areas, you are seldom more than an hour from the shelter a forest gives.

I love using a tarp when I am backpacking. A simple, good-sized rectangular 200-gram tarp made from lightweight material has served me well for over ten years. Complete with a nest underneath, it keeps bugs out, and the combined weight is 500–600 grams with pegs.

The best thing about this tarp and nest combo is that it is so well ventilated that it is almost condensation-free under most circumstances. It is also spacious and can sleep two in a pinch. It is my favorite shelter for forests and places like the California Sierras. It has stood up, battened close to the ground on a night in those mountains with sleet and high winds, right at timberline with only some crouching pine shrub around it.

I would not use this combination of tarp and nest on The Green Ribbon. Sure, it would be fine in the forest, and the weather above the tree line is not always rainy and windy, despite me harping about it. It can be glorious, as I hope some of the photos in this book show.

But to be safe, you should be outfitted for a worst-case scenario, and compared to the Sierras, Scandinavia is often rainy and windy. And when the really bad weather hits, I would not want to be under my tarp. I have pushed boundaries and traveled my mountains in bad weather with skimpy, homemade tarp tents and have no interest in repeating that experience. It is unpleasant, even if you are experienced enough to pull it off. So for the Green Ribbon I strongly advise you to use a tent. My experiences of tents along The Green Ribbon goes as follows:

Traditional Scandinavian double-wall tents have some crucial advantages over what I call American-type tents in rainy and windy weather. With American-type, I mean tents with a separate inner tent erected first and then covered with a rain fly. With Scandinavian tents, I mean those erected with the inner tent and outer rain fly connected.

This is a huge advantage if it is rainy and windy when you pitch the tent. Erecting an inner tent unprotected means that it might collect plenty of rainwater before you have the cover of a rain fly in place to protect it. In high winds, managing a vast rain fly and getting it solidly pegged in place can be quite challenging and take a long time, especially if you are alone. These American-type tents work better in a forested, continental climate with little precipitation, where they originate. A lovely thing about them is that you can pitch only the inner tent as bug protection on warm nights without rainfall. Great for sleeping under the stars in the Sierras but less likely to occur on the Swedish tundra.

Another thing to watch out for in a rainy country is what happens when you open your tent/rain fly door or doors. If you have a double-wall tent, the inner tent should have a vertical wall; the inner tent should not protrude into the fore-tent. What then happens is that rain can fall on the inner tent and its floor, making you sleeping area wet.

Scandinavian type double-wall tent. The sleep area is not exposed when you open the rain-fly door.

For a single wall tent, the same logic works. It should not expose your sleeping area when you open your door to get in or out. For this reason, I am not very fond of single-wall pyramid-shaped tents, so-called "mids," with a center pole. When you open the zipper to get in or out, almost half of your living area is exposed, rain might fall on your groundsheet or nest, making your sleeping area wet.

In brief, I recommend tents, single or double-wall, that can be erected in one motion, not exposing the inside to the elements. I prefer single-wall tents, which are usually lighter and where condensation on the inside is visible and can be wiped off. I also recommend that your tent has a fore-tent where you can cook and stow your gear, but with a vertical wall of fabric, or mesh, separating it from where you sleep. I would say that roughly two-thirds of my evenings in the Swedish mountains are spent cooking in my tent, either because of bugs or wind and rain.

The rain-fly, no matter if it is a single wall or double-wall tent, American type or Scandinavian, should preferably go down to within a couple of inches off the ground, all around.

When the rain-fly door is open the living area is often exposed to rain in this type of mid.

As for inner tents/nests, a mesh one will always be cooler, sometimes colder, than a solid fabric one. I have a homemade inner tent with solid fabric 50 centimeters from the ground up and then mesh. This protects my sleeping bag from the wind when sleeping, making a considerable difference temperature-wise. Still, it is cooler than a solid fabric inner, but on the other hand, I have better visibility. It is a compromise, and everyone makes their own choice.

All tents will have condensation inside on most nights in cool and wet conditions. I try to ventilate as much as possible; I always sleep with the door(s) fully open if there is little wind, even if it is raining (because my sleeping area is not exposed to vertical rain). Still, this does not entirely keep condensation away, neither for single nor double-wall tents.

It is often said that in double-wall tents, the solid fabric inner tent will keep the condensation away from you. This is not how it works in my experience. Perhaps because I am a tall person who uses small tents if I can, I always seem to press the inner tent against the outer with

Single wall tent in a great camp spot.

head, arms, or back, and my shirt or jacket will get wet. Not to mention the head and feet of my sleeping bag pressing the inner tent against the damp outer. I think this argument for double-wall tents is only valid if you are tiny or have a huge tent where you never risk pushing against the walls, bringing the inner and outer fabrics in contact.

The advantage of a single wall tent is that you can both see and reach the condensation and wipe it off. I usually start my day wiping and repeatedly wringing out a handkerchief-sized microfiber cloth before sitting up in my sleeping bag to start breakfast.

I know people have hiked The Green Ribbon with other kinds of shelters than those I recommend. It is, as always, up to you to make your own choices when it comes to gear. And take the consequences. Still, remember that there are plenty of suitable lightweight tents that will not weigh more than 1 kilo per person. Remember 343. Three kilos for the three big ones.

When I thru-hiked The Green Ribbon, my tent for the southern part weighed less than 500 grams. It was an early model from that manufacturer that turned out to have weaknesses when a rainstorm hit one night. The main problem was that the fore tent lacked a zipper, using pieces of Velcro tape instead. This did not hold in the wind. Also, the corner guy lines were too short and could not be adequately pegged and weighted down with rocks. This tent has since been improved on both aspects and would most likely work for the entire Ribbon.

For the northern part of the hike, my tent weighed 900 grams and was a well-tried trail companion. You see it on the cover of this book. Unlike the other tent, it also had solid nylon, not mesh, extending 50 centimeters from the ground up, to protect the sleeping bag from the wind. Brands and models of these two tents do not matter; it will change over time, and new models will evolve. I am just mentioning this to communicate that there are (in fact plenty of) tents that fit what I have described and recommend, which do not weigh more than 0,5–1 kilo per person.

Footwear

The most important, and most undeniable (there are, of course, people who deny it anyway), factor for long-distance hiking is that you should pick the lightest footwear that does the job. There is a lot of scientific research from the latter part of the 1900s, often financed by the US Army, proving the adage that "one pound on your feet equals five pounds on your back." In brief, it takes much more energy to lift and move weight on your foot than to transport the same weight in your pack. Some of these scientific articles you can read on my blog www.fjaderlatt.se. Just search for "weight on your feet."

So, whatever other choices you make, pick lightweight footwear for your Green Ribbon hike. Or for any hike.

I have touched upon footwear earlier in this book when writing about hiking in wet terrain. In my opinion, it is virtually impossible to hike for more extended periods in our Swedish mountains without your feet eventually getting wet.

Knee-high rubber boots are the only footwear I know of and have used for a couple of decades half a lifetime ago, that is genuinely and

For long-distance hiking in the Swedish mountains, mesh shoes have been my favorites for 20 years.

fully waterproof day in and day out. And still, you sometimes use them for wading water that is slightly too deep, and water runs over the top and into your boot.

Rubber boots have many disadvantages; they are cumbersome, hot, and sweaty in most weather. I do not recommend them. But the very fact that they are waterproof, and Scandinavia is decidedly wet and cool made them very popular among hikers for many years.

Another traditional type of footwear for Scandinavian hikers is the unlined leather boot with rubber covering the foot part. British troops discovered during the 80's that their regular leather boots were pretty crappy during the Falkland War in that south Atlantic wet and cold climate. This resulted in a significant order to a Swedish manufacturer of these rubberized leather boots. One advantage these boots have is that they are unlined, so they dry out faster than lined boots.

My experience is that your feet will get wet in these boots as well, but it takes longer than straight leather footwear. I used those rubberized boots in the army and hiking for many years but finally gave

Abandonded "continentals" found on the tundra.

up on trying to keep them waterproof and switched to knee-high rubber boots, as I have mentioned. This seems like ancient history these days, but I am saying it to motivate my experience that your feet will get wet hiking in the Swedish mountains.

Today, much motivated by fashion, many hikers here use what I call "the continental hiking boot." Those were initially made for the Alps and hikes in dry, rocky terrain. Used to ascend mountains, sometimes with crampons attached when walking on glaciers, they are often cumbersome and stiff. To compensate for the hardness and protect the skin of the feet, they are lined with foam and leather. Mainly they were used for day hikes and spent the nights indoors. These boots migrated to America, which has a lot of similar dry, rocky terrain.

These boots were not constructed for week-long treks at all and even less for hikes in a wet and boggy country, where they will spend their nights in damp tents, without any chance to get dry. Even if they were continuously treated with shoe wax and buffed to a shine, they were not waterproof for any duration. Once wet, the material and the linings soaked up water; they got even heavier and took days and nights indoors to dry.

Mastodons like these can still be seen in stores and on the trail. Fortunately, they are today being replaced by their children and grandchildren in the footwear family, boots made from lightweight materials and made waterproof by membrane linings like Gore-Tex and its competitors.

Despite these improvements in weight and water resistance, I would not use boots like these for longer, tent-based hikes in the Scandinavian mountains. This is because sooner or later, they will get wet. Usually sooner.

The biggest problem to my mind is that the waterproof membranes do not have a very long lifespan; they will eventually break and let water in. This usually happens long before the rest of the boot is worn out or even much worn. And since these boots are also lined with (absorbing) foam, they take forever to get dry. They are likely to remain damp if you are tenting, even if the weather turns hot.

Since it is such a hassle when these boots get wet, this explains why so many hikers along The Green Ribbon spend a surreal amount of time worrying about getting their feet wet and then suffering when they do, as I have already commented upon. In my opinion, membrane-lined leather, or fabric boots like these are unsuitable for The Green Ribbon.

It is much easier to embrace that your feet WILL get wet and choose footwear that manages being wet much better than lined boots. I recommend using low trail running shoes, preferably with lots of mesh in the uppers. They should be light and quick-drying, meaning they should have a minimum of padding and linings. I do NOT recommend such trail runners with waterproof membranes. They get wet and just take longer to dry than the unlined ones.

I have used a type of mesh shoe, almost without padding, for two decades of hiking in Scandinavia, northern Alaska, and Canada and found them the best compromise for wet country. In these shoes I wear very thin, synthetic socks which I find dries faster than woolen ones used by many hikers in trail runners. It is surprising how your feet can stay warm enough, even while damp, in low temperatures, as long as you are hiking with a pack and generating metabolic heat.

Sooner or later, the temperature will drop too far, or cold rain will be pouring all day. Then my feet get freezing in shoes and socks like this, and I need a backup. For this, I use waterproof socks with thick, insulating pile socks underneath. They are necessary in prolonged cold rain, and I would never go without having them in my pack. Heavy-duty plastic bags are a cheaper option since these socks with waterproof/breathable membranes are expensive and have a limited life span, just like boots with the similar waterproof membranes.

Blisters can always happen but seem to be much less of a problem with soft trail runners than with waterproof boots. I have had blisters once or twice, not more, after 15 years of backpacking in trail runners. It has occured after a lot of hiking on hard, unforgiving trails and even more unforgiving roads.

A vile and vicious triangle causes blisters: Friction, heat, and dampness. These should be minimized. Strangely enough, hiking boots instead seem constructed to maximise them.

Trail runners are softer than boots, causing less friction. Shoes without waterproof membranes also make your feet less warm and less damp.

Hey, somebody says: What about your feet getting and being wet in mesh shoes all the time? I would call that dampness!

Yes. Still, this dampness in a permeable mesh shoe does not seem to cause as much blistering as the kind of dampness ensuing from a damp or even wet foot and socks being almost hermetically ensconced in a waterproof boot. Feet like that tend to look like prunes and pieces of dead skin can sometimes be picked from them. That has never happened to my feet in mesh shoes. My guess is that it is the free passage of air that protects the skin.

Fact is that few things seem to be, literally and figuratively, as sensitive as feet. This also goes for talking about and recommending suitable footwear for hiking. Many people get outraged when they

Water-proof socks with pile socks underneath keep my feet warm and dry in rain and slush.

read my opinions above. A lot of hikers as well as, of course, boot manufacturers and their hired influencers/bloggers disagree. As usual, it is your choice, I can only relate my experiences.

If you take off on The Green Ribbon and change your mind about footwear after a week or two, it is usually easier to get hold of a pair of jogging shoes than a pair of hiking boots en route. During the Coast2Coast Sweden hikes that I arranged for several years, it was very common that hikers starting in boots switched to trail runners when we arrived in a town after some days.

You might be carrying double like many do, having a pair of runners in your pack for camp use and wading. While hiking the Bibbulmun Track in Australia, I encountered a hiker that had taped blisters on every toe. I am not exaggerating; I have photos to prove it. She had however brought a pair of running shoes and also flip-flops for camp use. I suggested that she switch to hiking in her runners, which she did. She never switched back to her boots during the three weeks we occasionally met up.

Clothing

I will describe the clothing I usually wear in the mountains and used on my thru-hike of The Green Ribbon. Since we just spoke of footwear and mentioned socks, let me start from my feet.

Inside my mesh footwear, I use thin nylon ankle socks, "ladies socks," 50 deniers or so, made from the same material and weave as ladies' stockings. I find they dry out faster than other socks, like those from thin merino wool. I use thin merino wool socks in dry, rocky country, like the High Sierras, but that is another story and other circumstances.

I wear lightweight, synthetic runner's pants on my legs, weighing 100–200 grams. They dry out fast and block the wind as well as bugs. Many people are unaware that thin microfiber pants are impenetrable to mosquitoes because of the tight weave. In heavier, coarser weave, "sturdy hiking pants," the moskers can wiggle their proboscis between the threads.

Drying time is essential; I can ford a creek with my pants on, and they are virtually dry in five-ten minutes, even if the sun is not basking down. Low weight is also good; when the weather is hot, I take them off, walk in my shorts, and the thin pants stuffed in my pack do not add much weight.

Shorts, yes. I use thin synthetic runner's shorts, weighing 100–150 grams, with a mesh inner brief. They do triple duty. They stand-in for my boxer shorts, I hike in them in hot weather and swim in them if I am in public areas. They are also easy to rinse and dry when the weather is nice, keeping them reasonably hygienic. They can get wet in prolonged rain and then dry faster than merino shorts, which I have also used.

I wear a short-sleeved merino polo shirt on my torso, with a collar. This is my base layer. I think it looks better than a t-shirt and turning up the collar gives some extra warmth at times. On top of this, I usually wear a thin windshirt that weighs less than 100 grams. Having a hood on this is essential for warmth and bug protection. A homemade baseball cap with a beak that keeps rain out of my face and sun out of my eyes is on my head. Thanks to that beak, I did not need to bring sunglasses on The Green Ribbon. I need both

Windshirt, runner's pants and mesh-shoes on a cold morning.

cap and sunglasses in sunny places with shining mountains, like the California Sierras.

For additional insulation, while hiking, I bring a thin, micro-fleece sweater (150–200 grams). It is often needed while hiking, when it is windy and rainy.

As a warm layer during breaks and in camp, I have a lightweight (200–300 grams) down or synthetic jacket with the essential hood. The hood adds very little weight and a lot of warmth. I use simple fleece gloves without a membrane; they dry faster. A lightweight fleece beanie for extra warmth dries faster than wool, and the fleece I am using is more wind-proof.

I use a lightweight (100–200 grams) rain jacket and rain pants of similar weight in the rain. Covering my fleece gloves is a pair of waterproof mittens (25 grams). You can use ordinary plastic bags for this, as well.

I have used ponchos/capes and find them suitable for protection from rain and minimizing condensation in forests on well-maintained trails. In the forest they snag when you hike off-trail and are not practical on the tundra. The wind catches them, which can be managed while hiking and in low winds but is very bothersome when setting up or breaking camp. I quickly got tired of hunching over tent stakes that had to be put into the ground, with the wind bringing the poncho up over my head, obstructing my vision, and exposing my back to the pelting rain.

I bring a hooded merino or synthetic base layer shirt and similar long underwear in my pack for night-time use. I also have a pair of dedicated night socks, only used in the tent, never in my damp shoes.

Almost all my clothing is made of materials that dry fast, which means thin synthetics. This is important for my well-being and to counter hypothermia when I spend days and weeks in a tent, with only my body heat to dry out wet gear. And I will get wet. I have yet to experience rain gear that has not leaked at the end of the day. I put my merino base-layer shirt in my pack when hiking in prolonged rain and wear the microfleece sweater next to my skin. Under really wet circumstances, dressing only in fleece and rain gear works best. But I still will get wet, it will only be more bearable, and the clothes will dry quicker.

On a day of rain, I usually put up my tent an hour or two earlier than usual because I am wet and cold after a day on the trail. After getting into the tent, I strip directly and put on my dry nightclothes, shirt, long johns, and socks. On top of this, I wear my damp day clothes, but of course not the wet rain gear. I then add my warm jacket, my puffy layer, pull my sleeping bag up to my waist, and start cooking.. I stick my feet into my sleeping bag, pull it up to my waist, and start cooking.

Depending on how wet things are and the outside temperature, I sleep in most of the clothes mentioned. I might take my now, from body heat, slightly drier day clothes off and sleep only in my nightclothes; it depends on how wet things have been and how cold the night is. Using this method, I will have reasonably, or entirely, dry clothes to put on for another day's hike come morning.

My usual first-aid kit; some band aids, tape and pain killers.

Safety

You will seldom be more than 10 kilometers in the Swedish mountains, as the crow flies from buildings or people. Along the more popular trails, there will be people and houses with food and heating at regular intervals. Many overnight huts and some rest huts have emergency radiotelephones that will put you in touch with the police and mountain rescue should you need them. It has never happened to me. You should be aware that these phones can be used for non-emergencies, like booking boat taxis across lakes.

Since this book unashamedly advocates taking the road less traveled, some precautions are advisable. Bringing a cell phone/device almost goes without saying, and I have already mentioned its use for GPS navigation. Most of us use the camera to record our outings to posterity, but you can also use it as a mirror when combing your hair or checking out splinters or whatnot in hard-to-see areas of your body. Still, you cannot rely on your cell phone to connect to your network. So, a good thing is to bring a small satellite device as backup.

My usual repair kit; dental floss and needles, tape, wire and safety pins.

If you are officially hiking The Green Ribbon, it is mandatory to bring an emergency transmitter of this sort. Development of these is rapid, and they can connect to your mobile phone for easier use, like sending text messages and e-mails. Stay away from devices that only allow one-way communication. Devices that only send messages but do not receive any confirmation from the addressee. This caused problems for me during a packrafting trip in Canada.

You will have to check the current rules on emergency transmitters and advice on models at The Green Ribbon website.

Always bring a few small things for medical care and repairs. The advice from medical professionals on this subject is not to bring stuff you do not know how to handle. For most of us, this means staying away from the substantial red bags sold through marketing by fear in many outdoor stores.

What I bring, and can handle, is some band-aids, some ibuprofen or other common pain killer. I also bring some more potent prescription painkillers should I get seriously injured. It has not happened so far.

A couple of meters of non-elastic sports tape is also good if you need to stabilize a sprained ankle. Also, I bring a couple of meters of brown 5 cm wide Leukoplast. This elastic tape can be used for blister prevention, closing gaping wounds (has never happened to me), and repairing things. I once used it in Canada to fix a tent ripped by a bear.

For repairs, I bring a needle and a length of dental floss for sewing, 20–30 cm of soft, thin steel wire, and some safety pins. Steel wire is very strong and can be used for tying things together, and the same goes for safety pins. The latter is, I think, underestimated. They are easy to use and will hold anything from ripped clothing to a damaged backpack waist belt together (has happened to me). I also bring some silver-colored duct/duck tape and a length of Tyvek Tape (not made of Tyvek, used to tape Tyvek in buildings) which is fragile but will stick to any synthetic fabric. It can tape rips and holes in clothing, rain gear, and tent fabrics (duct/duck tape does not usually stick to silnylon used in many tents).

This is not a gear book nor a book on hiking techniques, even if you are forgiven for thinking so, having read this far. I want to briefly touch upon things I believe are essential to give you a good experience on the trail. To make your hike as comfortable and safe as possible. I would like to finish this part with three personal gear choices for The Green Ribbon:

1. I would not hike in boots.
2. I would not hike without hiking poles; outstanding among rocks.
3. I would not use a tent/shelter that cannot be pegged close to the ground all around.

I am fully aware that other hikers have completed The Green Ribbon without following all or any of these points. In the end, it is up to everyone's personal choice.

Packrafts

As I write this, packrafts are becoming more and more popular and valuable for hikers. Packrafts weigh between 1–3 kilos, and with a paddle of less than a kilo and a personal floating device in the same weight class, this setup will add 3–5 kilos to a hiker's pack. For some people, this weight is worth the possibilities it opens.

Hiking along the many routes described in this book, you will find that the last ice age has carved depressions for numerous rivers that usually run from northwest to southeast, bringing the water from the mountains into the Gulf of Bothnia and then down to the Baltic Sea. Often these rivers run through big lakes and/or huge hydropower dams. So, many of the route suggestions in this book are about finding places where you can cross these significant waterways. You will need to use road bridges, rowboats, or boat taxis for some.

The packraft might change that. I have used packrafts on rivers and lakes in the Swedish mountains and northern Canada. This is what I have found.

A packraft works best flowing with the current. It takes a lot more effort to propel it forward on lakes than a canoe or a kayak. A bit of headwind, more substantial than a breeze, will make forward progress next to impossible, no matter how hard you paddle. Of course, it is just the opposite with the wind at your back.

With no unfavorable winds, you can cross sizable waters with a packraft, but I recommend being very careful. If you are paddling for hours on a big lake, the weather might change and turn nasty. A very lightweight, cheaper type of packraft might have difficulties managing this. Even if you have a sturdier, white-water capable packraft, you need to have the skills yourself to manage high waves. Something you only get by packrafting a lot.

Packrafts are ideal, in my opinion, to cross smaller lakes, rivers, and creeks that are not fordable. A stream should be reasonably slow-moving, unless you are skilled, and you need to learn ferrying techniques for this. Ferrying means that you point the front end of the packraft some 45 degrees upstream and paddle in that direction. This will compensate for the current and bring you, more or less, straight

Preparing to packraft a corner of Lake Virihaure. The "personal floating device" is by no means certified by any authorities.

across from where you started. If you attempt to paddle straight across, the current will carry you downstream from your goal.

At the time of writing, the packraft is not a common sight along The Green Ribbon, and there are no route suggestions in this book that demand the use of one. Maybe in the future.

How to behave

You will find information about how to behave responsibly on your trek at The Green Ribbon webpage. The thing to remember is that you are moving through country where people live and work, and respecting that. The entire area is Sami country; the reindeer you encounter is domestic and owned by someone.

The Sami people have been living in this area for a long time, and they have special rights in connection with reindeer management. Most noticeable will be the right to erect buildings, build fences and drive motorized vehicles like quads and motorcycles on the tundra. Fences can be found around a big, more or less round enclosure, called "rengärda" on the maps, where the reindeer are gathered. Fences can also be many miles long, blocking your way, built to keep reindeer from one Sami village mixing with those from another. A Sami village is not a village as such but an economic and administrative union in a specific geographical area. The members have the right to manage reindeer husbandry in this area. There are usually gates in those fences between Sami villages on well traveled trails. You have to find a place to crawl under or climb over them in other areas.

The reindeer you encounter will be mostly smaller flocks. If you encounter hundreds or even thousands of animals, they are probably being gathered by their owners and driven towards the enclosures,"rengärda." Often, helicopters together with men and women on the ground are used to drive the animals. In those cases, you must take extreme care not to interfere with their work. Scattering a herd that has been gathered during days and nights of hard work is not something you want to do.

For the same reason, I advise you not to pitch your tent near a fenced-in "rengärda" used for gathering purposes. It might be prepared for use. More information can be found at www.laponia.nu.

Generally, you should adhere to the Leave-no-trace principles of camping. If you are not familiar with this, you should search the Internet. It is nothing complicated, just common sense. Unfortunately, common sense is not always very common. We are talking primarily about not changing or damaging the nature you hike through. The ideal is that there should be no trace of you ever visiting a place.

Another thing you should think of is not to set up camp in somebody's backyard. The Swedish Law of Common Access gives you a right to walk and camp pretty much where you want, but not to disturb people where they live.

Do not leave "tent rings" after you.

Do not build new rock cairns as trail markers or rock rings around fireplaces. This is a Boy Scout practice. The Sami themselves have not done that, nor do they. They start a fire without any construction work except gathering fuel.

You will encounter a number of rock ring fireplaces on your trek. If there is such a one, though, build your fire there. Please do not make a new rock ring next to it. Unfortunately, in these fireplaces, you will also discover that many hikers have never learned that aluminium packages do not burn. Do not make that same mistake.

Sometimes, you need to anchor your tent pegs and guy lines by putting rocks on them in high winds. From a leave-no-trace view, the best thing is to take stones out of streams and then put them back in the stream in the morning. Do not leave these rocks in a ring when leaving, as a certain indication of there having been a tent. Put the stones back where you took them or scatter them around.

I sometimes take the time to scatter the rocks of little-used fire rings and especially "tent rings" that I pass, to leave the place as pristine as possible for future hikers.

Another bunch of things should also be common sense. You pack out your trash. You do not wash upstream from where somebody might be taking drinking water. Do not clean your dishes and cooking pots in lakes or streams. Instead, fill your utensils with water, scrub them, and scatter the dirty water over biologically active ground (where things are growing).

There are books written on how to shit in the woods. What I have read is not particularly adaptable to a tundra situation. You will find no big leaves with which to dry your butt. A bunch of grass might sometimes be found and can be used, but it will likely leave residues that might cause chafing between your buttocks. Use toilet paper, but do not bring a whole roll. Pick up a meter per day or whatever suits you at your resupply points and keep it in a plastic bag.

Bringing a pocket shovel for digging a cat hole has also turned out to be of little use for me. They work well in many areas, like in America, where the ground is often dry and sandy. On the tundra, you will find rocks, vegetation, and roots that make it pretty much impossible to dig at all in most places.

This is how I manage my fecal needs:

I search for an earthbound rock, the size of a shoebox or a bit bigger. Half of it, perhaps, is underground, but it can be pried, lose and lifted, leaving a nice depression. I squat over this hole and get the job done. Then I set fire to the used toilet paper in this hole. In a wet area like the Scandinavian mountains, the risk of starting a fire when you have absolute control over a few pieces of paper is almost non-existent. If any plants or roots near the hole should begin to smoulder, I step on it thoroughly, extinguishing every spark.

When this is done, I replace the shoebox rock the way I found it. I then disinfect my hands with gel, also kept with the tissue and lighter in the same plastic bag. I do this right away to sanitize my hands before digging with grubby hands into my bag of trail snacks. It is easy to infect yourself and then of course blame the water or the food...

Poop hole.

Trail sections and route suggestions

Rules for The Ribbon

This has already been mentioned, but in brief, The Green Ribbon is a trek through the mountains between Grövelsjön Tourist Station and the Three Country Cairn (Treriksröset). Those points mark the ends of the Swedish mountains, the fells. You can start at either end; if you are going north, you are northbound, a NOBO, to use expressions coined on American long-distance trails. Going south from Treriksröset, you are a SOBO, southbound.

You can walk the entire Green Ribbon, you can walk parts thereof, or simply use some of the route suggestions in this book as an inspiration for shorter or longer treks not connected with The Green Ribbon. But if you choose to be an official part of The Green Ribbon trek, you must sign up at their website and pay the fee. That is how you get the diploma to hang on your wall.

Since rules may change and this book may not, once it is printed, I will not go into detail about the rules here. Everything you need will be found at the White and Green Ribbon website: www. vitagronabandet.se. However, this is to give you a rough idea of what to expect:

To keep hikers in the mountains, instead of, say, walking the highway along the Gulf of Bothnia, the rules stipulate you will have to pass west of a handful of landmarks along the mountain range. You will have to check what these landmarks are on the official website.

You will not be allowed to use motorized transport (but you can use a bike), except boats across major lakes. You also must bring an approved emergency transmitter. You are not allowed to start a Green Ribbon attempt very late in the season for safety reasons.

The rules allow you to hitch-hike or take a bus or taxi for medical care or resupply, but you must return to the exact spot where you

Meadows blooming in early summer near Medstugan in Jämtland.

boarded the magic carpet and continue your trek uninterrupted on foot from there.

Statistics from the first decade

The Green Ribbon officially started in 2011, and some statistics for the first decade, or rather the first 11 years, might be helpful. Things will probably change as more and more people take the challenge, and the latest statistics will be found on The Green Ribbon website.

Between 2011-2021 375 hikers have officially started a Green Ribbon thru-hike, and around 60 percent were men and 40 percent women. 265, about 70 percent of the hikers starting also completed their hikes. Women and men were both just as likely to complete.

Of the 375 hikers starting, 235 were NOBOs (northbound, started in Grövelsjön), and 140 were SOBOs (southbound, started at Treriks-röset). Both groups were just as likely to complete the trail; perhaps the NOBOs (27 percent) were slightly less likely to abort than the SOBOs (33 percent).

Around June 15, the number of hikers starting from Grövelsjön (NOBO) increases considerably and remains high for the next 2–3 weeks, tapering off towards mid-July.

The number of SOBOs starting from Treriksröset rises considerably about a month later, around July 15, and remains relatively high for the next couple of weeks. However, the pattern for SOBOs is less distinctive, the number of starters being spread out over almost the entire hiking season.

To sum it up, most thru-hikers start from Grövelsjön and walk north in the latter part of June. That is what I did and one reason for me to write the route descriptions in this book from a NOBO perspective.

Logistics for The Green Ribbon

Hiking The Green Ribbon will entail a certain amount of logistics. You must plan when you are going to start and where. You must know how to get to the starting point. You must know what to bring with you. You must plan your food resupply points.

Travel to the start (and from the endpoint) depends on where you come from, and communications will change over time, so I will not go into details here. The Internet will be up-to-date and help you.

Winter is long in the mountains, and basically, there is a time window from mid-May to mid-October. That is stretching things quite a bit (I would not start that early or expect to finish that late unless I bring skis), and you might end up with a lot of snow in one or both ends and be unable to complete your hike. Recommended is mid-June to mid-September.

Most Ribboners are NOBOs, starting in Grövelsjön. The advantage is that spring and snowmelt come earlier in the south than 1000 kilometers to the north. So you can start hiking earlier in the season from the south.

If you are flexible timewise, I would recommend starting your hike between June 20-30 in the south, from Grövelsjön, and then walking north with spring. Myself, I started from the south on June 19. If you cannot start that early, perhaps because of work constraints, starting from the north on a later date might be better. Since winter

Early summer – lots of water.

begins later in the south, it is better to finish at Grövelsjön than Tre-riksröset late in the season.

If you run into trouble with your body and feet or gear, this usually happens early in your hike. Starting from the south means many huts with hosts, other hikers, and villages with road access to help you. If you start from the north and use The Swedish Route, there is almost nothing of that kind for the first week or two, should you need to bail out for safety reasons. If you go through Norway from Treriksröset, there are more huts and support.

How many days you will be hiking depends on many things but mainly on the route you choose and the distance you walk daily. If you pick the shortest route, which involves quite a bit of road walking, the distance is about 1300 kilometers. If you, as I did, try to avoid roads and maximize time spent in the more beautiful and exciting parts of the mountains, it will be about 1400 kilometers. Or more if you like.

Mount Cokcu dominates the wetlands on The Cap of the North.

Competing for the fastest time on The Green Ribbon is not encouraged, and your diploma will state the number of days, not hours, from start to finish. Trail runners have covered the distance in around 20 days. I spent 60 days doing 1400 kilometers on the Ribbon, including about a week of short distance days and complete rest days. The average daily distance for my hike was 23 kilometers (26 kilometers if I only count the days spent hiking and not the rest days). I consider this, and myself as a hiker, to be neither slow nor fast. I am not young, which slows me down, but I have a light pack that helps me stumble along.

If you compare the above to your physical status, pack weight, the experience of long-distance hiking, and ambitions, you have the beginning of a plan. Some people have spent almost 100 days hiking The Green Ribbon. Going fast or slow is all up to you and what you want to experience. Perhaps it is a great experience to spend 100 days in the mountains and running The Green Ribbon in 20 days is an awful one. Or it might be just the other way around. People are different, which I find rather nice. Try to find what suits you and to hike your own hike.

Picking the most exciting route suggestions from this book, you can sum them up and find how long your version of The Green Ribbon is likely to be. Divide this by the daily distances you can manage, put in a suitable amount of rest days, and have a time span.

Once you know how long you will be on the trail, you have to plan how long it will be between places where you can resupply. Resupplying is almost all about getting food for the next part of your hike. However, you might also want to change some of your gear during your trek, either because it breaks down or because you need, for instance, a warmer sleeping bag and clothing towards the end of your hike.

Your food preferences will affect your logistics quite a bit. There are two extremes: you buy everything as you go, or you send all your food ahead to pick up points. Or you do a little bit of both.

I bought everything along the trail because I did not want the hassle with sending boxes and because I enjoy combining the food I find in different stores into something that will fuel me on the trail. Sometimes that meant eating things that I did not really like, but hunger is always the best spice.

Another reason was that I am an omnivore; I can eat everything. If you have allergies or preferences, like being vegan, you cannot rely on finding what you need in many of the small stores you will be passing. Or perhaps you simply like to dry and package your own trail food.

As a rule, mountain lodges/tourist stations and similar have stores selling things like freeze-dried food, gas canisters, and other stuff for backpackers. However, a small, general store in towns and villages might not have those things, so you must plan accordingly. Freeze-dried food might be replaced; my favorite way is using mashed potato powder combined with vacuum-packed sausages. Finding gas canisters for your stove might be a problem in a village store; alcohol for stove use seldom is.

If you do not buy everything along the way, you will have to send boxes to different places. This is quite a logistic challenge which you might enjoy, or not. Sending food packages means you must calculate the number of days between different locations to where boxes can be sent and then find someone willing to hold your box. These can be campgrounds, hostels, mountain lodges, stores, or even private individuals (trail angels). The Internet will give you up-to-date information (which a book like this cannot) on what possibilities exist in places along your route and how to contact them ahead of time. Some might charge you a bit for holding your box; others will do it as a service if they get your business. If you rely on a store to hold a box or to buy food in, remember to check if it is open on Sundays, should you plan to pass on such a day.

In some areas, you will only be a couple of days of hiking between possible resupply places, but in others, you might have to carry food for 7–10 days, depending on your route and speed.

There will be information on The Green Ribbon website and the corresponding Facebook group for most of the above.

Kungsleden and Nordkalottleden

Kungsleden, in English correctly translated as The Royal Trail but also called The King's Trail, is more than 400 kilometers of trail between Abisko and Hemavan. Most hikers on The Green Ribbon use it because it is convenient and usually the shortest route. Many parts of it are also very beautiful.

There are several guidebooks on Kungsleden in different languages, and more will probably be published. You will find a current list at the end of the book. Therefore, I will be pretty brief when describing Kungsleden in this book. Another reason is that I find it a bit over-populated and would rather have Green Ribbon hikers discover alternatives. You will also miss a lot of beautiful country if you hike only on Kungsleden. The good news is that you can have it both ways, walk the best parts of Kungsleden and the best parts off Kungsleden.

This book will describe several other routes that will connect with Kungsleden in different places, enabling you to pick a Green Ribbon route of your own that combines the best areas in the Swedish mountains.

Nordkalottleden, The Arctic Trail (not to be confused with The Arctic Circle Trail on Greenland), is some 800 kilometers of hiking between Sulitelma in Norway or Kvikkjokk in Sweden, through

Kungsleden near Aktse, with magnificent Skierfe to the right and Sarek beyond the Nammasj cube.

Sweden and Finland to Kautokeino in northern Norway. 350 kilometers of the trail is in Sweden, and Nordkalottleden intersects with Kungsleden and Padjelantaleden in places. For Green Ribboners, the most useful part of Nordkalottleden is the one offering a shortcut from Abisko/Tornehamn, through Norway, to Treriksröset. Many hikers on The Green Ribbon use that part of the trail. Like with Kungsleden, there are blogs and books about Nordkalottleden in different languages, so I will also be pretty brief about that route suggestion in this book and focus on the roads less traveled, the ones on the wild side.

Via Suecia

Via Suecia is a long-term project started by a bunch of enthusiasts aiming to create a Swedish National Scenic Trail. The idea is to establish a trail from the southernmost part of Sweden, at Smygehuk on the Baltic coast, to Treriksröset. The northern part of Via Suecia goes through the mountains, and there it connects with or could be used as a means to hike The Green Ribbon.

Via Suecia aims to be a designated, well-marked trail like Kungsleden with trail blazes between Smygehuk and the Treriksröset. It will probably be a long time before that is realized, but there is a virtual trail (which will most likely change over time until the physical trail is in place) that can be downloaded as maps and GPS files from the website www.viasuecia.com.

The virtual trail makes use of existing trails to a large extent and includes a lot of road walking. It will coincide with several of the route suggestions I give in this book. I will not particularly comment on this since the Via Suecia route is a work in progress, and the virtual trail may change considerably over time.

Time can change everything

One of my motives for writing this book is to steer hikers away from the paved and most boring parts between Grövelsjön and Treriksröset. To inspire you to have a much better experience of nature and wildlife. Perhaps also a much better connection with your own life. This does not mean that what you read in this book is the gospel, and the trail to salvation is trusting every word I have written. The world is not quite like that, and neither is this book. There is, above all, something called Time.

I wrote this book based on my experiences when I hiked a particular route and on decades of crisscrossing the Swedish mountains. It might not be the same as what you encounter on your hike along the same route. Particularly not if you hike it one or five or twentyfive years after this book is written. Which is 2022.

Some areas and trails described can and will have changed. Plants grow, and trees fall. I am sad to say that many trails I have described are poorly managed by the authorities responsible and not always easy to find. However, this also changes with time. The route I could not find last summer might be rejuvenated entirely this summer. It might be rerouted next summer.

Also, there is the question of seasons and weather. The trail I describe from walking it in early summer might be different for you,

Not a favorite of mine, road walking.

walking in late summer. The ford I described as of medium difficulty might be manageable or impossible for you a month, week, or even a day earlier or later. The view I describe as magnificent may be invisible due to rain and fog.

This book contains almost 3000 kilometers of route alternatives through Sweden and Norway between Grövelsjön and Treriksröset. I have not walked every kilometer of every route. I do not even want to walk some of them and would be happy if you did not walk them either. I am mainly talking about roads, some of which I have driven by car.

However, since Green Ribbon hikers use these routes, they must be included in a book like this. I have received detailed information from hikers who have used them.

So, you cannot rely solely on me or this book for your hike. You need to get good area maps, digital or printed, preferably both.

My route suggestions are, literally, suggestions. What you will experience along this route is up to the season, weather, people, and circumstances and how you manage these on your very own hike.

Evening at Alggajavrre, one of the westerly gates into Sarek National Park.

Maybe that is even why you backpack. To experience your own unique life to the fullest. To grow as a person as well as a hiker. To listen to the sounds of your own feet whispering on the leaves of the crowberries. To see the sun roll away behind peaks sprinkled with snow while every muscle in your legs is achingly happy. Instead of spending your days watching someone else's life on a screen, with your ears plugged from the sounds of your own life.

A few things about maps and place names

I will primarily use the words and spellings you will find on a map over the mountains between Grövelsjön and Treriksröset. These placenames will usually be in the Swedish and Sami languages. In some cases, I will attempt translations into English. There are several different Sami languages you will encounter and some Finnish place names in the northernmost part of Sweden.

The Sami languages were not written. As cartographers were visiting more and more of northern Sweden in the late 1800s and early 1900' s, place names on their maps were written in Swedish, based on what the Sami pronunciation sounded like to a Swedish speaker.

Many of these spellings on maps have been replaced by a modern, more phonetic spelling, attempting to be more faithful to the Sami pronunciation.

Place names on maps in the Sami languages often give information about the character of these places. This can be very useful for a hiker; it gives you an idea of what to expect. To help foreign hikers, I have made a brief list of Swedish and Sami words you will encounter on a map and translated this into English.The descriptive terms can be found as suffixes at the end of a place name. So Visttas-vaggi means the Visttas Valley. Unna Visttasvaggi is the small(er) Visttas valley.

Some Swedish words used on maps and otherwise are also helpful to know. Most place names in the southern half of The Green Ribbon hike are Swedish.

The determined article is always added to the end of a word in the Swedish language. "Stuga" means hut, and "stugan" means "the hut." "Stugorna" is plural and means "the huts," indicating that there will be several buildings at a site with overnight huts, like at Sälkastugorna.

For the Norwegian part of Nordkalottleden, it is helpful to know that
"hytte" means hut.

Sami	English
Bakti, bakte, pakte	Rockwall. Gaskkasbakti.
Cohkka, tjåhkkå	Mountain peak. Gaskkascohkka.
Eatnu, ätno	River, usually not fordable. Rapaätno.
Gorsa, gårsså	Ravine, canyon. Beaivvegorsa.
Javri, javrre	Lake. Vuoskkojavri.
Jiekna, jiegna, jeagna	Glacier. Vuojnesjiegna.
Johka, jåhkå	Creek, usually fordable. Tjåggnårisjåhkå.
Luokta	Bay. Staloluokta.
Vaggi, vagge	Valley. Visttasvaggi.
Stuora/stuorra, stuor	Big. Stuor Jierta.
Unna	Small. Unna Visttasvaggi.

Swedish	English
Affär	Store, usually food store.
Bensinstation	Gas/petrol station.
Berg, berget	Mountain, the mountain.
By/byn	Village, the village (usually small, but can be as big as a town).
Bäck/en	Creek/brook, the creek/the brook. Usually fordable.
Dal, dalen	Valley, the valley.
Led, leden	Trail, the trail.
Myr, myren	Marsh/bog, the marsh/the bog.
Rengärda	Reindeer enclosure (fenced in area).
Renvaktarstuga	Reindeer herders hut (almost always locked).
Sjö, sjön	Lake, the lake.
Stuga, stugor, stugorna	Hut, huts, the huts.
Vindskydd, rastskydd	Wind shelter, rest hut, rescue hut.
Väg	Road.
Å, ån	Creek, the creek. Bigger than a brook, smaller than a river. Often fordable.
Älv, älven	River, the river. Big, seldom fordable.

Blåhammarens Fjällstation in Jämtland, a classic STF mountain lodge.

Other sources of information

The White and Green Ribbon is administered on www.vitagronaban-det.se. Lots of information to be had on their website, which as time goes by will be much more up to date on many details than this book. Fortunately, the mountains and valleys I describe are more eternal.

Google Maps is handy for exploring towns and villages, searching for hotels, hostels, campgrounds, stores, and other things you might need. For lodging, searching sites like Booking.com and Airbnb is also a great help.

Lantmäteriet (The Swedish Mapping, Cadastral, and Land Registration Authority) is a government agency in Sweden that provides information on Swedish geography. They have online maps and aerial photos that can be very useful. I have used their maps extensively when calculating distances and writing this book. Their website is www.lantmateriet.se, and you will find free, downloadable maps here: https://minkarta.lantmateriet.se/.

Rough weather in Sarek, one of the areas getting the highest precipitation in Sweden.

Lantmäteriet themselves has ceased to publish printed maps and Metria now runs this business. They publish the classic Fjällkartan, which is found in many stores online and in real life. There are two other publishers of mountain maps, Calazo at www.calazo.se and Outdoorkartan (outdoorkartan.se). Both print their maps on Tyvek or similar materials. I find Tyvek maps lighter, more durable, and better adapted to my needs than the classic Fjällkartan.

The Swedish Tourist Association, STF, is a pioneer organization that opened the mountains for tourism long ago by building trails, lodges, and overnight huts. They still manage many huts and lodges that you will encounter along the mountain range. They have lots of information on the mountains at www.svenskaturistforeningen.se/.

Laponia is a UNESCO World Heritage which includes the national parks of Sarek, Padjelanta, and Stora Sjöfallet. More information at www.laponia.nu. Many huts in this area are managed by Badjelannda Laponia Tourism (BLT); you will find information on this at www.padjelanta.se.

Sections

I have chosen to describe the routes from south to north, NOBO because that is the most frequent choice for Ribboners, and the direction I used on my thru-hike.

The route descriptions are divided into five major sections, numbered 1–5. Maybe someone else would have sliced the sausage differently. Perhaps they have only helped me structure my thinking, but they do connect, and I believe they will help you plan your hike. This does not necessarily mean a Green Ribbon thru-hike. They can be used for planning shorter hikes in nice areas, with information on road access and other useful factors.

Although sometimes they do, the five sections do not necessarily end or begin at towns or other natural trailheads. However, a P for Parking on the maps indicates access by road to a place. The general idea is that the sections have several separate routes that come together again where a section ends.

In each of the five sections, many alternative routes are described. They have names based on where they start and where they end. They are also numbered to make navigating among them more accessible. The first figure is the section number; the second is the route number. Route 2.2 will be the second route described in Section 2 and named Storlien – Anjan.

The separate route descriptions in a section follow a mold. At the beginning of each description, there is a frame. First, in this frame, you get the total distance; then, you get this divided into distances between significant waypoints listed vertically. Those are usually huts and rest huts but might also be trail forks, bridges, major road crossings, farms, villages, or towns.

Having the distances between the waypoints written vertically between the waypoints makes it easier to read. No matter if you are reading them from top to bottom or from the bottom up like you will do if you are a SOBO instead of a NOBO.

You might discover differences in distances given in this book compared to other sources—for example, other guidebooks, online information or signs along the trails. Trails can also be re-routed. I

0
100 km
Treriksröset
Section 5
Abisko
Bodø
Stora Lulevatten
Torneälven
Kalixälven
Kvikkjokk
Hornavan
Luleälven
Section 4
Storavan
Hemavan
Luleå
Storuman
Skellefteälven
Skellefteå
NORWAY
Gäddede
Section 3
SWEDEN
Umeå
Section 2
Östersund
Örnsköldsvik
Helags
Section 1
Härnösand
Grövelsjön

hope these differences will not amount to more than a kilometer or two, plus or minus, but they should not affect your trek much.

After the distances between waypoints, you get the "Effort"headline. This could be Low, Medium, or High and indicates my subjective estimation of the physical effort needed along this route. This is primarily due to many ups and downs, more or less steep, on a segment. One very steep incline and nothing more might still be considered Low. Many steep slopes would not be a Low. However, the descriptions are always given for a hiker walking north. It might be less or more strenuous to hike it towards the south in some cases. As usual, a topographic map will give detailed information.

The headline "Skills" will then follow. This can also be graded Low, Medium, or High and refers to the hiking skills I subjectively believe a route will demand. Low usually means that the trail is well marked and easy to follow; there is plenty of rest huts, overnight huts, and plenty of other hikers. You probably can do without a tent or navigation skills, and there are bridges at major creeks and boardwalks across the marshlands.

High skills, finally, mean that there are no or few trails, no or few huts, and no or few bridges. These are what I like to call the walks on the wild side. The extent of these segments will be described in the text.

Finally, inside the frame beginning every separate route description, the headline "Summary" gives a brief take on the route and its connection to other routes.

After this frame of condensed information about a route, you get a shorter or longer text describing what you might encounter along the trail and information on lodgings and resupply options. Well-traveled trails like Kungsleden and Nordkalottleden, which others have described in detail in books, blogs, and whatnot, get a comparatively cursory description. Off-trail hiking through areas less well known get more loving care from me.

I have felt it prudent to add coordinates to a location in some instances. This is usually not an obvious waypoint, like a hut or a village, but a place, road, or path that is more obscure. These coordinates that can be entered into a digital map system are all WGS84 and use the decimal degree system.

SHORTEST ROUTE OR GREATEST ROUTE FOR A THRU-HIKE

I will give you a few pointers before diving into all the different route suggestions. It all depends on what you are looking for. One thing might be the shortest, and probably fastest, way of doing the entire Green Ribbon using the route suggestions in this book. Here it is. There are probably shortcuts that will shave some kilometers here and there. But from the routes that I have described, this is the shortest combination:

No	Name	Km
1.1	Grövelsjön – Rödfjället	66
1.2	Rödfjället – Hamra – Klinken	35
1.4	Klinken – Helags	26
2.9	Helags – Vålådalen	42
2.11	Vålådalen – Ottsjön – Undersåker	32
2.12	Undersåker – Vike/Olden	82
2.13	Vike/Olden – Rötviken	52
2.14	Rötviken – Valsjöbyn	17
2.8	Valsjöbyn – Murfjället – Gäddede	58
3.1	Gäddede – Raukasjö – Klimpfjäll	101
3.3	Klimpfjäll – Hemavan	141
4.1	Hemavan – Tärnasjöstugan	37
4.2	Tärnasjöstugan – Ammarnäs	40
4.3	Ammarnäs – Jäkkvik	91
4.4	Jäkkvik – Kvikkjokk	88
4.5	Kvikkjokk – Saltoluokta	72
4.6	Saltoluokta – Abisko	135
5.1	Abisko – Tornehamn – Pålnostugan	20
5.5	Pålnostugan – Nordkalottleden – Treriksröset	147
	Total kilometers	1 282

You might not be looking for the quickest way to do The Green Ribbon, but perhaps the nicest, with the best scenery and the most rewarding wilderness experience. Below you will find my favorite. It is almost, but not quite, the route I followed on my thru-hike (see next page).

No	Name	Km
1.1	Grövelsjön - Rödfjället	66
1.2	Rödfjället - Hamra -Klinken	35
1.4	Klinken - Helags	26
2.1	Helags - Storlien	55
2.2	Storlien – Anjan	76
2.4	Anjan – Skäckerfjällen – Gaunälven	44
2.5	Gaunälven – Tjovre – Rötviken	93
2.14	Rötviken – Valsjöbyn	17
2.8	Valsjöbyn – Murfjället – Gäddede	58
3.2	Gäddede – Sutme – Klimpfjäll	113
3.3	Klimpfjäll – Hemavan	141
4.1	Hemavan – Tärnasjöstugan	37
4.7	Tärnasjöstugan – Vuoggatjålme	104
4.8	Vuoggatjålme –Staloluokta	115
4.9	Staloluokta – Aktse	97
4.5	Aktse – Saltoluokta	33
4.6	Saltoluokta – Alesjaure	100
4.12	Alesjaure – Katterjåkk	47
4.13	Katterjåkk – Pålnostugan	30
5.3	Pålnostugan – Vuoskojaure	73
5.4	Vuoskojaure – Kummavuopio – Treriksröset	100
	Total kilometers	1 460

You might not be looking for a thru-hike in one or several years but simply want some ideas of shorter hikes in pleasant surroundings. Then you can browse the different routes that follow in the book and pick what suits you.

UPPER: View of Stor-Rensjön towards Skäckerfjällen, Jämtland.
LOWER: Basstavagge, a high alpine valley in Sarek.

Section 1: Grövelsjön – Helags

This section is straightforward, with few alternative routes from the start in Grövelsjön to Helags Fjällstation/Mountain Lodge, which is in the middle of the tundra, some 15 kilometers from the nearest road.

I recommend that you start a thru-hike from Grövelsjön instead of Treriksröset, if you can. The trails are well-marked and there are plenty of huts and other hikers. A great segment for making you used to the trail.

The suggestions for Section 1 are described in the route numbered 1.1–1.4 and the total distance is about 125–130 kilometers, depending on which routes you select.

Mount Helags dominates the hike from Klinken towards Helags Mountain Lodge.

Steinkjer
Murfjället
Lobbersjön
Gaunälven
Grubbdalen
Valsjöbyn
Rötviken
Skäckerfjällen
Kolåsen
Anjan
Kallsjön
Olden
Strömsund
Storlien
Åre
Undersåker
Ottsjön
Vålådalen
Storsjön
Östersund
Helagsfjället
1 796 m
Helags
Klinken
Hamra
Tänndalen
Rödfjället
Grövelsjön
NORWAY
SWEDEN
Sveg
0
50 km
1

1.1 Grövelsjön – Rödfjället

Total distance: 66 km

Distances between waypoints:

⇨ Grövelsjön, mountain lodge

20 km

⇨ Storrödtjärnstugan, overnight hut

17 km

⇨ Rogenstugan, overnight hut

17 km

⇨ Skedbrostugan, overnight hut

12 km

⇨ Rödfjället (trail junction)

Effort: Low to Medium. Some long climbs, not steep. Very rocky in places.

Skills: Low. Navigation easy, overnight huts and rest huts available, tent not necessary.

Summary: The beginning of The Green Ribbon is on well-marked trails, gravelly, sometimes very rocky. Plenty of huts for overnight use about 20 km apart. The trail junction on Rödfjället will give you a choice of two routes. One via Hamra/Fjällnäs (1.2), the other via Tänndalen (1.3). Both alternatives will later meet at Klinken.

Communications to Grövelsjön are by car or bus, the latter often in combination with trains. The fjällstation/mountain lodge at the end of the road is run by STF (Swedish Tourist Association) and has a restaurant and lodgings and a small store with trail food and some hiking gear.

If you are officially on The Green Ribbon, it all starts by placing your hand on the blue front door. You look at the map on the wall and check out the names of hikers who have previously completed the Ribbon, and then you are off. If you are a SOBO, arriving from the far north and Treriksröset, it is a place for celebration: a shower, a five-course dinner, and a night between clean sheets.

Soon after leaving the blue door you are on the tundra, which will be the case for most of the well-marked trail to Storrödtjärn-

Grövelsjön Mountain Lodge, where The Green Ribbon begins or ends.

stugan. The exception is around Lake Hävlingen, where you will find some trees. The overnight hut at Storrödtjärn is also run by STF and has beds, a kitchen, and a host operating a small store during the high season in summer. This is the standard for almost all STF overnight huts and hut places (some have more than one house) you will encounter.

Soon after starting my hike, I saw this little pine striving on the tundra.

North of Storrödtjärnstugan, you enter Rogen Nature Reserve, where the land is a unique moraine creation from the latest ice age, some 10 000 years ago. For the hiker, its main feature is that it is incredibly rocky and hence detrimental to speed hiking. I found hiking poles to be very helpful to avoid a twisted ankle that would have endangered the entire trek. Lake Rogen will become more and more prominent, with stunning views in good weather as you approach Rogenstugan. You do not need to walk up to this hut; on a topographical map you see the shortcut.

Otherwise, Rogenstugan is an overnight hut run by STF and has beds, a kitchen, and, during summer, a host operating a small store. There is a trail leading east to roads and civilization in the village of Tännäs, but most Green Ribbon hikers prefer to stay west of this area and remain in the mountains. That trail follows Lake Rogen for quite a ways.

Camp at Lake Rogen.

Close to the Norwegian border, the trail turns right and heads for Skedbrostugan. This is another hut run by STF, with a kitchen, beds, pit toilet, and, in summer, a host operating a small store.

By the bridge at Myskelvadet, a beautiful place, you find flat spaces among the birches for at least 50 tents. This is seldom encountered in the Swedish mountains. You will often be happy to find a flat space for a single, tiny tent between the rocks or trees. The trail then climbs the shoulder of Rödfjället, where the routes chosen by Green Ribbon hikers often differ. The right-hand trail takes you by Tänndalen; the other path goes by Fjällnäs. Both routes will be described in the following, and they will come together at Klinken.

On this part of the trail, I meet several hikers who, like myself, had started on a thru-hike of The Green Ribbon. I never saw any of them again, probably because we chose different routes and held a different pace. The hut hosts were also used to hikers with their mind set on Treriksröset.

1.2 Rödfjället – Hamra – Klinken

Total distance: 35 km
Distances between waypoints:
⇨ Rödfjället (trail junction)
  14 km
⇨ Hamra, store
  13 km
⇨ Långbrottstugan, bridge
  8 km
⇨ Klinken, bridge

Effort: Low. Well marked trail, some road walking.

Skills: Low. Navigation easy, villages and rest huts available.

Summary: You will go through Hamra from the trail junction at Rödfjället. There is a store in Hamra, which could serve as your first resupply after Grövelsjön. There is lodging in both Hamra and nearby Fjällnäs. At Klinken you join the route Rödfjället – Tänndalen – Klinken (1.3). Both routes are the same length.

The left-hand trail on Rödfjället (WGS84 62.490417, 12.268444) will take you across the tundra with lovely views of Svansjön below. To the west, out of sight, is Lake Bolagen, where I did some fishing during my first trip to the mountains at at age thirteen. I did not catch any fish; instead, the mountains got me hooked for life.

At the north end of Svansjön, the trail brings you east and to the top of the ski lift. A road will take you down into the forest to a bridge across Tännån and right by the store. There is a camping site as well as lodging nearby.

Leaving Hamra, you follow small roads towards the northwest that will take you to the trail system and the bridge across Anderssjöån (not the road bridge). You continue through the forest, passing a rest hut before the trail moves towards the tree line. The path then dips down again and passes east of V Kroktjärnen and another rest hut before hitting the tree line anew, this time with a steeper climb up to and across Långbrottfjället. The trail then descends towards the rest hut and bridge close to Långbrottstugan,

There is a steep climb up to a nice plateau from this bridge, taking you north and then down to the bridge over the river Ljusnan, at the beautiful area around the old but well-kept farm buildings and meadows at Klinken.

Meadows at Klinken.

1.3 Rödfjället – Tänndalen – Klinken

Total distance: 35 km

Distances between waypoints:

⇨ Rödfjället (trail junction)

   8 km

⇨ Tänndalen, bridge

   9 km

⇨ Svalåtjärn, rest hut

   5 km

⇨ Bruksvallarna, village

   8 km

⇨ Ösjöstugan, seasonal café

   5 km

⇨ Klinken, bridge

Effort: Low, apart from the long climb out of Tänndalen.

Skills: Low. Navigation easy, villages and rest huts available.

Summary: This is the route if you take the right hand trail on Rödfjället (WGS84 62.490417, 12.268444), and it will also take you to Klinken. You pass close to Bruksvallarna, which could serve as a first resupply after Grövelsjön. At Klinken you join the route Rödfjället – Hamra – Klinken (1.2). Both routes are the same length.

The left-hand trail on Rödfjället will take you to Hamra and Fjällnäs, but you are taking a right and will have excellent views of the green valley at Tänndalen, with Hamrafjället rising above it. This mountain is worth a visit for those botanically interested. With vast numbers of plants and flowers in bloom in early summer, it is a fantastic place.

You more or less walk down the ski slope into Tänndalens Stugby, with lodgings and a cafè. They will probably hold a box for you if you stay overnight. You then follow the road in a long bend, crossing first the river and then the main road. The nearest grocery store is at Hamra, 7 km of road walking to the west. If you want to shop there, you should take the route described for Rödfjället - Hamra - Klinken.

You cross the main road in Tänndalen and pick a steep gravel road, which takes you to a parking lot at timberline. A broad trail takes you across the tundra to Andersborg, a nice café without road access. You can grab something to eat and drink. Limited hours of operation, though.

Continuing, you will come to Svalåtjärn rest hut. You might skip Bruksvallarna if you are not resupplying there. Instead, you hike straight ahead towards Klinken.

If you go to Bruksvallarna, the trail is downhill all the way. After about 5 km, you come to a system of roads that will lead you to the center village. Bruksvallarna is a ski resort, perhaps more for Nordic skiing than for the downhill variety. It has several places that offer lodgings and a grocery store open year-round (the store at nearby Ramundberget is probably not open year-round). However, stores and opening hours might change, you must check this on the internet.

The same goes for lodgings; check on the Internet at sites like Hotels.com or Airbnb. Most lodgings will probably hold a resupply box for you for a fee or if you stay the night.

Leaving Bruksvallarna, you follow the trail uphill until you reconnect with the trail you left at Svalåtjärn rest hut about 5 km north of

Snow bridges, often unreliable, often helpful.

Snowmelt and high waters in June.

this hut. There are, in fact, several routes you can take from Bruks-vallarna, including a road to Klinken. As usual, I recommend staying away from the roads. Instead, you should take the trail that brings you through the lovely valley along the Ösjön lakes. I spent a pleasant, sunny couple of hours dodging between patches of snow, doing their best to melt and reindeer, doing their best to get out of my way.

Before leaving the tundra, you will connect with the route suggestion via Hamra/Fjällnäs. The trail descends for another couple of kilometers into the forest and then comes to the bridge across the river Ljusnan. This is one of many significant rivers you will cross going north. Here it is still tiny. Klinken is the name of the well-kept old farmhouses on the river's north bank.

Old Sami style goahti rescue hut at Rödfjället.

Caption

1.4 Klinken – Helags

Total distance: 26 km

Distances between waypoints:

⇨ Klinken, bridge

6 km

⇨ Svaaletjahke, rest hut

8 km

⇨ Svalåtjärn, rest hut

5 km

⇨ Fältjägarstugan, overnight hut

12 km

⇨ Helags, mountain lodge

Effort: Medium. A fairly steep climb from Klinken, a medium climb north of Mittån, and also when approaching Helags.

Skills: Low. Well-marked trail, overnight huts, and rest huts available, tent not needed.

Summary: This is a beautiful part of the hike, with great scenery around mount Helags. From Helags, you have a significant choice between what I call Jämtland West and Jämtland East. Those two main routes meet in Gäddede some 300 kilometers north, even though you can switch between them in places.

Going steeply up from the meadows and lush vegetation around the Klinken, the trail leads to a ford after about 2 km. This ford is likely to be the first of any distinction since the beginning of your hike. It is a reasonably easy ford but could be of greater difficulty in early summer or during/after prolonged rains.

A nice hike across the tundra follows the ford, with primarily low hills around. To the left, Skarsfjället is more substantial, and Helags will continue to grow impressively on you on the horizon.

You will pass the rest hut at Svaaletjahke and then head downhill towards the creek Mittån. This ford is also easy most of the time. There are some nice camp spots on both sides of the stream.

A long and fairly taxing uphill trek will follow after the ford, and then it is pretty flat going to Fältjägarstugan, which can be seen from far away. Fältjägarstugan is a hut run by STF and has beds, a kitchen, and, during summer, a host operating a small store. The original hut site was built to commemorate three soldiers who died nearby in a snowstorm in 1944.

The trail continues with easy hiking across the tundra; Mt Helags is now utterly dominant on your left. A fairly steep climb will take you across Ö Helagsskaftet, through a reindeer fence, and then down towards Helags Mountain Lodge. This is a significant operation run by STF, with several buildings, restaurant, huts with self-service kitchens, and a relatively well-stocked store. I had cell phone reception when I passed. There is no road to Helags.

Walking to the top of the mountain Helags itself is a day trip that can be recommended. It was my first experience of a view from a significant peak in my teens. I still remember the ache in my thigh muscles that night.

At Helags Section 1 ends, because deciding if you are going left or right from here will have consequences for a week or two. It is about choosing between Jämtland East and Jämtland West, described in Section 2. They are very different, West being mountains and quite a bit off-trail hiking, East being forest and a lot of road walking.

Camp at Svalåtjärn.

To where the path leads — Helags.

Section 2: Helags – Gäddede

This section of the hike offers more alternative routes than Section 1. But no matter how you choose, you must pass through the small town of Gäddede in the northern part of the province of Jämtland. I have chosen to describe two alternative routes from Helags to Gäddede, which I call Jämtland West and Jämtland East.

Jämtland West is described in routes 2.1–2.8 and the approximate distance is 335–350 kilometers. Jämtland East, described in routes 2.9–2.15 and is roughly 285–300 kilometers. Jämtland West might take two-three days longer to hike for an average hiker. You can switch between East and West in a couple of places

A significant difference between West and East is roads. I define them as anything between a logging road and a highway. This definition is a bit flexible, but I would say that Jämtland West has about 70–100 kilometers of road walking, which means 25–30 percent of the entire distance. Jämtland East has about 140–160 kilometers of road walking, or about 50 percent of the entire distance.

Jämtland West has a lot more hiking on tundra mountains, Jämtland East is mostly forest. Jämtland West has more off-trail travel and fords, demanding or developing better hiking skills. It also takes more physical effort since the roads on Jämtland East are less exhausting to walk, albeit harder on the feet and legs.

My opinion is clear. I have found Jämtland West one of the best parts of the entire Green Ribbon. I have not walked many of the roads along Jämtland East, but I have driven some of them. I also have no interest in walking those roads, but they are chosen by many hikers on The Green Ribbon. Probably partly due to lacking awareness of the alternatives.

Your choice: Mountains or forests, off-trail or on roads, fewer days of hiking?

Something that makes the decision easier might be that you can switch between Jämtland West and Jämtland East in some places. And all routes eventually lead to Gäddede, where you can share your highs and lows with other Green Ribboners

Klimpfjäll
Slipsikstugan
Raukasjö
Sutme
Tunnsjøen
NORWAY
SWEDEN
Gäddede
Murfjället
Lobbersjön
Steinkjer
Gaunälven
Grubbdalen
Valsjöbyn
Rötviken
Skäckerfjällen
Kolåsen
Anjan
Strömsund
Kallsjön
Olden
Åre
Undersåker
Storlien
Ottsjön
Vålådalen
Storsjön
Östersund
Helagsfjället
1 796 m
Helags
Klinken
Hamra
Tänndalen
Rödfjället
Grövelsjön
0
50 km
2

2.1 Helags – Storlien

Total distance: 55 km

Distances between waypoints:

⇨ Helags, mountain lodge

   11 km

⇨ Miesehketjahke, rest hut

   9 km

⇨ Sylarna, mountain lodge

   10 km

⇨ Enkälen, rest hut

   8 km

⇨ Blåhammaren, mountain lodge

   13 km

⇨ Storvallen, main road E14

   4 km

⇨ Storlien, village

Effort: Low to Medium. A couple of fairly steep climbs south and north of Sylarna. Downhill from Blåhammaren.

Skills: Low. Well-marked trail, overnight huts/lodges, and rest huts available, tent not needed. Lots of hikers.

Summary: This is a beautiful and classic route in the Swedish mountains. You pass Sylarna and Blåhammaren, well known mountain lodges managed by STF. Storlien is a good place to resupply. Once in Storlien, it is very difficult to connect to Jämtland East before Anjan (2.3).

Going West or East, starting at Helags, is a significant decision between a slightly shorter route with lots of road walking, mainly in the forest, and a slightly longer way with beautiful mountain scenery. Here we go West, the routes along Jämtland East will be described separately (2.9).

The route west from Helags towards Sylarna is easy walking in the shade of the mighty Helags. It is the highest mountain you will encounter for a long time, until Lapland. You are heading for another impressive collection of peaks, Sylarna, only slightly lower than Helags.

The walking is easy until you have passed the rest hut at Miesehtjahke. The trail then starts to climb and becomes relatively steep towards the pass 1 km south of Sylarna Mountain Lodge, managed by STF.

This fjällstation/lodge has lodging and a reasonably well-stocked store, considering it is a long way from the nearest road. Which understandably makes things expensive. I would not resupply here since it is only a short distance to cheaper and fully stocked grocery stores in Storlien. On my thru-hike, I only bought some chocolate and a Coke.

From Sylarna, you head downhill, crossing the creek Enan on a bridge, and then take the left-hand trail towards Blåhammaren. There is initially a fairly steep climb towards Endalshöjden. After having passed the Enkälen rest hut, you are on a flat, usually wet, tundra's expanse with long boardwalks. You hike slightly uphill until you reach Blåhammaren, another STF classic lodge.

The buildings at Blåhammaren have an old-time flavor that I like. I have been there several times, in summer and winter. Once, I slept out front in a tent during a winter storm to save money and see if the tent would handle the wind. This had a friend, who had slept inside, come out to the half-buried tent in the morning and tremblingly ask if I was alive.

Helags Mountain Lodge.

The lodge is famous for its fruit soup, and you can have dinner there if you like, although residents might fully book this before you arrive. If you hike east, there is another STF lodge, Storulvån, where there is road access. Hiking from Storulvån to Sylarna to Blåhammaren and then back to Storulvån has become an initiation for many hikers in Sweden. This, the Jämtland Triangle, is often recommended as a good hike for first-timers in the mountains.

As a thru-hiker, you will generally have no business in Storulvån. Instead, you head down the steep trail beginning right behind the lodge at Blåhammaren. The path levels out fairly quickly, and you enter the birch forest, crossing the creek Enan for the second time since you left Sylarna.

Following the trail over the rounded mound of Rundvalen, you then descend to Storvallen, where there is a road and lodging. After a brief walk on Highway E14, the trail leaves the main road and continues, mostly on minor roads, into the village of Storlien.

You will find accommodation and stores in Storlien. It is an excellent place to resupply. In the early 1900s, the new railway brought tourists to Storlien, and downhill skiing was introduced. The Swedish king used to ski in the area, and Storlien was a popular resort for a long time, beginning to fade in the late 1900s. Today it is a pleasant backwater that has retained a bit of old-world charm and seems like a poor relative to the very expansive and bustling World Cup ski resort of Åre, to the east. If you go on Jämtland East, it passes along the eastern fringe of Åre.

On my thru-hike of The Green Ribbon, Storlien was my first resupply after leaving Grövelsjön. I bought food in Storlien to last me until Gäddede, or so I thought. Unfortunately, I had been over-optimistic about my pace and ran low on food. Fortunately, I could buy enough food in Rötviken to last me to Gäddede. If you do not send boxes ahead to places in between, I would buy supplies in Storlien that will last to Rötviken.

UPPER: Sylarna Mountain Lodge. LOWER: The Sylarna massif.

2.2 Storlien – Anjan

Total distance: 76 km

Distances between waypoints:

⇨ Storlien, village

   17 km

⇨ Medstugan

   8 km

⇨ Norra jaktstugan

   8 km

⇨ Storrensjön, farm

   9 km

⇨ Lill-Rensjön, dam

   5 km

⇨ Melen, road, farm

   13 km

⇨ Anjan, mountain lodge

Effort: Low to Medium. Few severe ups and downs. Off-trail hiking is pretty straightforward and even inviting.

Skills: Medium. Navigation skills and tent needed. Few people, but roads and houses are seldom far away.

Summary: This is a favorite route of mine for The Green Ribbon. Some easy off-trail hiking with lovely views and some interesting old buildings along the way. Anjan is a possible place to send a box. The nearest store is in Rötviken. From Anjan you can switch to Jämtland East (2.3).

You follow a well-marked trail uphill from the center of Storlien across Skurdalshöjden towards Åhlénstugan (rest hut). Before you reach that hut, you leave the summer trail and head in an easterly direction, north of the hut and north of the winter trail. This will be running on your right, but it often goes across bogs and marshland, so you are better off picking a route higher and drier, up along the south slope of the hill Rensjövalen.

You stay at about 700-750 meters above sea level, follow this topographic curve around Rensjövalen and then head north, east of another hill, Flatrun. It is easy walking and with beautiful views of Norder-Rensjön, the big lake to the east, and the forests beyond.

You aim for the buildings at Rensjösätern (closed) at the northern end of Norder-Rensjön. From Flatrun, you ascend diagonally towards those buildings. Just aim for where the creek ends and the

Rensjösätern and the bridge.

lake begins. There is a bridge across the creek, right by the buildings, which is not on the map. Rensjösätern is a beautiful, well-kept place that stands out with its pink colors in the middle of all the green, far from other habitations. It is one of several similar places in the area built as hunting lodges in the late 1800s.

From Rensjösätern, you pick a trail that soon attaches to the winter trail towards Södra Jaktstugan (closed) and then follows it down into the forest to Medstugan. This is another hunting lodge from the same era as Rensjösätern. Medstugan is run as a hostel, has road access and they might hold a resupply box for you.

You follow the main road from the buildings for about 400 meters to the north and then take the nice wide path going uphill towards Norra Jaktstugan (closed). When you reach that hut, it is time to bring out your navigation tools again.

You aim for the road that ends at the Storrensjön farm, straight north of Norra Jaktstugan. The hiking is easy and not as wet as it looks on the map. The best route is staying on elevation and hitting the road about 2 km from the farm. Passing north of Långklumpen, you avoid the steep terrain and arrive at the road.

You follow the road almost up to the houses at Storrensjön and then pick the path leading northwest to lake Sausjön. From that lake, you head towards the easternmost, very narrow little bay of Lill-Rensjön. Going across from Sausjön to Lill-Rensjön is easy walking and not as wet as the map might indicate. Stay on the moors for as long as possible and then follow the lakeshore from the little bay. Your goal is the dam at the northernmost bay of Lill-Rensjön, where there also is a house (locked) (WGS84 63.673889, 12.437917).

The dam makes this route from Storlien to Anjan easy. Otherwise, this area is blocked by big lakes and significant creeks that might

Lake Äsingen, near Anjan.

not be easy to cross. Some Green Ribboners use an option to walk close to the border and sometimes into Norway. This choice, however, eventually means a lot more road walking as you make your way from the border to Anjan.

A wide path will take you down from the dam to the farm Melen and the main road from Norway. You will be walking this road, which is not heavily trafficked, all the way to Anjan.

Anjan Mountain Lodge is an extraordinary place with lots of charm. It was built by Eyvind Frölich in 1937 in a rustic North American style, complete with totem poles, inspired by the time Frölich spent as a trapper in Alaska. Ensure the hotel is open and check what services they provide if you plan to visit. They will probably hold a box for you. It is an out-of-the-way place, not discovered by many, and might not last as a commercial enterprise.

2.3 Anjan – Skäckerfjällen – Kolåsen

Total distance: 35 km

Distances between waypoints:

⇨ Anjan, mountain lodge

    10 km

⇨ Strydalen, rest hut

    8 km

⇨ Sockertoppen, rest hut

    6 km

⇨ Rutsån, ford

    11 km

⇨ Kolåsen, mountain lodge

Effort: Low to Medium. Some road walking and some steep climbs.

Skills: Low. Marked trails and rest huts. One ford of medium difficulty.

Summary: This is also an excellent route and another favorite of mine: It goes through Skäckerfjällen, through the most alpine setting, including a high pass, you will have encountered so far. Going down to Rutsdalen is beautiful, and the hotel at Kolåsen has food and lodgings. From Kolåsen, you will face everything from a bit (2.6) to a lot of road walking (2.7), depending on the routes you pick.

From Anjan, you follow the main road for about 4,5 kilometers until you reach the northbound trail towards the Strydalen rest hut. You ascend steeply through the forest. Once above the tree line, the path gets less steep. The scenery all around is beautiful. Looking south, across the woodland, you see the big lake Kallsjön, as well as numerous other lakes, fade into the distance. Ahead, you are entering the Skäckerfjällen mountains. This is a small but precious alpine area with little-visited peaks and valleys.

From the Strydalen hut, you climb steeply through a pass and descend, also steeply, into the valley with the Sockertoppen rest hut. On my second visit to that rest hut, I realized it was 30 years since my first visit. The wet and dreary October snow made me switch from hiking in rubberized leather boots to high rubber boots for several years. This was before I discovered the advantages of hiking in trail runners, complete with waterproof socks for things like October snow. On this second visit to the hut, I also realized that one single piece of gear had been with me on that visit 30 years earlier – my cooking pot.

You can connect with the route suggestion described in the section Anjan – Skäckerfjällen – Gaunälven (2.4) by taking the steep but rewarding pass one kilometer west of the Sockertoppen rest hut.

Staying on the route to Kolåsen, however, you take the trail east, down to the forest and a ford across Rutsån, running through the beautiful valley of Rutsdalen. As you trudge along this small river, it changes its name to Storvallån. At the Storvallen farm, you connect to the minor road that will take you to the Kolåsen Mountain Lodge.

Kolåsen has food and lodgings and might hold a box for you. If Anjan is closed, this might be an alternative resupply point en route from Storlien. From Kolåsen, you can connect to Jämtland East using the route Kolåsen - Olden/Vike (2.7). If you remain on Jämtland West, you can connect with the route described in Gaunälven – Tjovre – Rötviken by using the route Kolåsen – Tjovre (2.6).

Going downhill into beautiful Rutsdalen valley.

2.4 Anjan – Skäckerfjällen – Gaunälven/Gaunan

Total distance: 44 km

Distances between waypoints:

⇨ Anjan fjällstation

10 km

⇨ Strydalen, rest hut

7 km

⇨ Sockertoppen rest hut, about 1 km west of

7 km

⇨ Rutsälven, ford

12 km

⇨ Burvattnet, ford

8 km

⇨ Gaunälven/Gaunan, ford

Effort: Medium to High. Some steep climbs and much off-trail hiking.

Skills: High. Navigation is tricky at times, but not so much with a GPS. Several fords, one of which is unpredictable: no overnight huts, few or no people.

Summary: This is a rewarding true wilderness trek, but demanding. I have hiked it twice (parts of it three times), from both north and south, and it is worth the effort. It continues with the route Gaunälven – Tjovre – Rötviken (2.5) to which you can connect from Kolåsen – Tjovre (2.6).

From Anjan, you can choose between continuing the wilder Jämtland West collection of routes or switching to the Jämtland East routes, which contain more road walking.

If you have no resupply scheduled for Anjan or Kolåsen but plan to resupply at Rötviken, you do not need to go to Anjan. On my Green Ribbon thru-hike, I left the road from Melen at the southern end of lake Äsingen and traveled cross country west of lake Njietsjaevrie. I continued north of Lake Mansjön and took the pass close to the Sockertoppen rest hut, going north into Rutsdalen. You can also use the road to Ottsjö läger (a Sami camp) and continue off-trail.

However, if you start from Anjan, you had better follow the route described under Anjan - Skäckerfjällen - Kolåsen. About one kilometer before reaching the Sockertoppen rest hut, you leave the trail

The totem pole at Anjan Mountain Lodge.

and head straight north over the steep pass between Opmedstjahke and Skeavratjahke. This is hard work, but the views are great on both sides of the pass.

Coming down from the pass, you aim roughly for the depression between the hills Bielnie and Dueljienasie on the north side of the creek Rutsälven. You descend at an angle into Rutsdalen and ford the slow-moving Rutsälven at a suitable spot, keeping in line with the depression west of Bielne. The suffix "-älven" indicates a more substantial waterway than a creek, namely a river, but Rutsälven is not very big. When I first forded it many years ago, the old map called it "Rutsån," signifying a smaller waterway, which is more correct.

After passing between Bielnie and Dueljuenasie, you need to take some care to find your way into the not very prominent valley east of Burvattsklumpen. You will now be traveling cross country to where the river Gaunälven/Gaunan enters the vast lake (actually a hydropower dam) of Torrön. I recommend that you first aim for lake Burvattnet, right on the Norwegian border. There are some huts (closed) there. You ford the creek Binnan at a suitable place close to where it exits the lake.

From Burvattnet going north, you can use the path indicated on the map, it might not always be easy to follow, but the walking off-trail is also reasonably comfortable. Bogs, of course, but you are far away from the well-kept tourist trails.

Your goal is to reach Gaunälven a bit from where it flows into Gaunviken, upstream from the hut (closed) on the south bank. Walk to the narrowest part of the river. That will be almost 600 meters as the crow flies northwest of the hut (WGS84 63.981472, 12.729389).

At times Gaunälven is easy to ford at that place. You can walk on a rocky ledge if the water is low; it will be no more than knee-deep in places. However, it is impossible and even dangerous to try this if the water is high since it moves with great force across this ledge. Do not try to ford here if you cannot see the rock ledge above water in several places.

I have crossed Gaunälven twice. Once, it was an easy ford, and the second time, I had to swim. I did this a couple of hundred meters

Sometimes Gaunälven is easy to ford.

upstream from this narrow spot with the rocky ledge. How to do a swim like that is described in another chapter in this book.

There might be another option, to cross Torrön by boat. The people living at the small farm of Edevik have shipped some Green Ribbon hikers across. This is easier to arrange hiking from the north to the house at Edevik. Coming from the south, you must arrange this before leaving Anjan (or where you have cell reception, do not count on having it standing on the shore of Torrön).

Most boat transports along The Green Ribbon rely on the good-will and physical presence of people living in the area when the hiker arrives. The Green Ribbon Facebook group is an excellent place to check things like this.

Having crossed Gaunälven, you might need to catch your breath. You can then continue on the route Gaunälven – Tjovre – Rötviken (2.5). Using roads from Edevik, you might also connect with Jämtland East by the route Kolåsen – Vike/Olden (2.7).

Sometimes Gaunälven is not so easy to ford. I swam across here.

2.5 Gaunälven – Grubbdalen – Rötviken

Total distance: 93 km

Distances between waypoints:

⇨ Gaunälven, ford

  11 km

⇨ Edevik, farm

  3 km

⇨ Holdern, road bridge

  21 km

⇨ Tjovre, bridge

  5 km

⇨ Lill-Burvattnet, dam

  22 km

⇨ Grubbdalsån

  13 km

⇨ Höberg, farm

  3 km

⇨ Logging road

  10 km

⇨ Rörvattnet, camping site

  5 km

⇨ Rötviken, store, lodgings

Effort: Medium to High. Some steep climbs. Lots of cross-country hiking.

Skills: Medium to High. Navigation is sometimes tricky. Several fords of minor or medium difficulty. Few trails.

Summary: This is one of the best wild country passages among my route suggestions between Grövelsjön and Treriksröset. Off-trail hiking means that some of the distance given between waypoints might not apply to everyone. This route takes you across two trail-less mountain areas, Sösjöfjällen and Offerdalsfjällen, and down a beautiful forest reserve, Grubbdalen. This entire route is a favorite of mine, but at times challenging. At Tjovre route 2.6 from Kolåsen connects.

After having crossed Gaunälven, do not try to follow the shore of the lake Torrön toward Edevik; it is incredibly steep and thick with living and dead trees and bushes. It will make you weep.

Walk by the hut called Gånälven on the map and then make your way towards the northeast. Keep climbing, avoiding the ravine along the creek coming from Gaundalsfjället. You follow that tundra ridge after reaching the tree line, still going roughly northeast until the terrain becomes less steep around the stream Hösjöbäcken. You cross

The hut named Gånälven.

that creek and swing south, staying on elevation (you will descend gradually), following the path of least resistance across the moors. You will sooner or later run into a quad trail, not on the map, that will take you to Edevik. It runs relatively close to lake Torrön for the last bit before you see the houses.

From Edevik, you follow the gravel road to the bridge at Lake Holdern and then to the main highway, which you cross for some more walking on the wild side.

Ahead you have Sösjöfjällen, which you will cross off-trail because there are no trails and hence no or few hikers. Your next goal is the dam at the southern end of lake Lill-Burvattnet. That dam will let you pass the two big lakes blocking your way.

After crossing the road near Holdern, you climb towards the tree line, more or less following the creek Tvärån and its branches. You aim to hike just south of the mountain Stapeln/Ohtje Tjalnge. This rough and rocky country is a wild walk. Then you continue east, south of the mountains Kyrkan and Stoere Tjalnge, and work your way south of Majkstjahke, towards the creek Fisklösån.

You follow Fisklösån towards the Sami camp at Tjovre, close to Stor-Mjölkvattnet. From Tjovre you take the trail across the bridge and head north along the trail to the dam marked on the map.

After crossing the dam at Lill-Mjölkvattnet, you have another collection of mountains without trails ahead, Offerdalsfjällen. You head in a north-easterly direction to reach the beautiful valley of Grubbdalen.

The easiest route to Grubbdalen I have found to be along the lakes under the sheer wall of Bielnie. Approach the lake Jillie-Bielnienjaevrie from the west and follow the south shores of the lakes. Then head north of Plyöjhkere and down to Grubbdalsån. Crossing Offerdalsfjällen south of Mehkene is an option but more challenging.

Grubbdalen is a valley of old forests, bogs, and moors. It is a nature reserve, and rightly so. You ford the sizable but slow-moving creek and follow the northern bank downstream to Höberg. The closer to habitation, the more and muddier quad tracks you will encounter.

Höberg is an old farm with a lovely view from the front door, now owned by a fishing association. You follow the path leading east until you hit a logging road; in time, that will become a major, hardtop road that takes you to Rörvattnet, where there is food and lodgings at a camping site. I was lucky; they had bear burgers on the menu. They will probably hold a box for you, but it is more practical to send a box to Rötviken, further down the road. There you will find a well-stocked store and a camping site with lodgings just across the road.

At Rötviken, you connect with the route from Vike/Olden (2.13) and the collection of route suggestions I have called Jämtland East. You follow 2.14 to Valsjöbyn where West and East will divide again into routes 2.8 and 2.15.

Höbergstjärnen in Grubbdalen valley.

The camping site at Rötviken - across the road from the general store.

2.6 Kolåsen – Tjovre

Total distance: 38 km

Distances between waypoints:

⇨ Kolåsen, mountain lodge

   8 km

⇨ Ytteräng, bridge

   15 km

⇨ Väg till Sösjövallen

   15 km

⇨ Tjovre, bridge

Effort: Low. Road walking and off-trail, few ups and downs.

Skills: Low to Medium. Navigation off-trail from Sösjön to Tjovre.

Summary: This route takes you to Tjovre, letting you connect with the route from Gaunälven to Rötviken. It is an excellent alternative if you do not want to cross Gaunälven/Torrön (2.4). The route from Tjovre and onwards is described in Gaunälven – Tjovre – Rötviken (2.5).

From Kolåsen, you can choose between the route suggestions I call Jämtland West respectively Jämtland East. The first alternative, via Tjovre, involves a bit of road walking; the second route from Kolåsen to Olden/Vike (2.7) means massive road walking. Thankfully much of it is on small gravel roads with little traffic.

Both route alternatives start with you walking from Kolåsen to Ytteräng and the road bridge. Heading along Jämtland West to Tjovre, you take the road north. Just follow that road for 15 kilometers and then take the road, and then the path, to Sösjövallen. From there, you navigate the valley northeast to Tjovre. You might encounter quad tracks in connection with the rengärde.

The route onwards from Tjovre to Rötviken is described under Gaunälven-Tjovre-Rötviken (2.5).

Looking towards Skäckerfjällen.

Cabin at Tjovre.

2.7 Kolåsen – Vike/ Olden

Total distance: 43 km

Distances between waypoints:

⇨ Kolåsen, mountain lodge

   8 km

⇨ Ytteräng, road bridge

   35 km

⇨ Vike/Olden

   (WGS84 63.693778, 13.659333)

Effort: Low. Road walking, mostly flat.

Skills: Low. Road walking, some houses, and traffic. No overnight huts.

Summary: This route is all on (small) roads and will lead you from Jämtland West to Vike/Olden, connecting with Jämtland East (2.12).

This route takes you from Jämtland West to Jämtland East at Olden/ Vike. You walk east from Kolåsen and reach a road bridge at Ytteräng. From Ytteräng, you follow a long and winding, narrow gravel road through dense forest with few houses for 35 kilometers. Fortunately, the traffic is limited on this road. At Olden/Vike, you meet 2.12 and turn north on a small road (WGS84 63.693778, 13.659333) and continue on the route described in the section Olden/Vike –Rötviken (2.13).

A lot of gravel roads to Vike/Olden.

UPPER: Nice forest camp. LOWER: Small brook with good drinking water.

2.8 Valsjösbyn – Murfjället – Gäddede

Total distance: 58 km

Distances between waypoints:

⇨ Valsjöbyn, village

8 km

⇨ Gunnarvattnet, road

8 km

⇨ S Penningkejsen, end winter trail

15 km

⇨ Avansbäcken, ford

11 km

⇨ Storvattnet, hut (locked)

8 km

⇨ Murunäset, farm

8 km

⇨ Gäddede, village

Effort: Low to Medium. Some ascents, off-trail hiking. Some road walking.

Skills: Medium to High. Lots of cross-country hiking with route finding. A couple of fords of medium difficulty.

Summary: The route to Valsjöbyn is described in Rötviken - Valsjöbyn (2.14) and is the same for Jämtland East and Jämtland West. This route via Murfjället on Jämtland West is lovely, the downside being some 18 kilometers of road walking in total. The country is nicer and wilder than the slightly longer Lobbersjön (2.15) alternative, which has about 40 kilometers of road walking. In Gäddede, there is lodging, a camping site, and a resupply store.

From Valsjöbyn, you follow the winding road towards Gunnarvattnet. After about 2 kilometers, you pass the road to Vinklumpen and the route via Lobbersjön. In Gunnarvattnet, you walk past most houses until you see a road going off to the right (WGS84 64.123222, 14.132250).

This road will quickly become a path, climbing through the forest, taking you east of Säterhögen. The trail is well marked towards Penningkejsen, a noticeable mountain right on the Norwegian border. You follow the winter trail marking, red wooden X:s, across most-

The trail from Gunnarvattnet.

ly dry moors. This trail ends in a depression below the rock face of Penningkejsen.

From the depression, you climb towards the shoulder of N Penningkejsen and the saddle west of Skaalnge. The top of that pass gives you beautiful views of the country north. You continue straight north from there, aiming for the eastern shoulder of Murfjället. Choosing your route around lots of small ponds and lakes on this route, you ford Kroesshbielienjohke/Tvärån, which should be easy. If seemingly impossible, there is a bridge some 4 kilometers downstream. That is where Jämtland East passes, and you can switch to this route, Valsjöbyn – Lobbersjön – Gäddede (2.15).

You continue up the valley between Murfjället to the west and Bierniekliehpie to the east. Staying fairly close to Murfjället should keep you away from most of the willow thickets.

You are heading for where Avansbäcken crosses the Norwegian border. There, maybe 100-200 meters east of the border, you will find

UPPER: Cairn marking the border towards Norway. LOWER: The Avansbäcken ford.

a wide, reasonably flat area where crossing Avansbäcken should be a ford of medium difficulty. (WGS84 64.303194, 14.142806)

After fording, you keep east of Spååjme and then continue north, almost right on the borderline, for about 10 kilometers. You pick your route between the small lakes dotting the tundra. In this area, I ran across a guy who was not satisfied with only hiking The Green Ribbon but was walking from the southernmost part of Sweden to Treriksröset on his private version of Via Suecia.

The course will take you between Akkarumpen and Sjulter-klumpen until you reach the lakes around Storvattnet. From the huts (closed) at that lake, you take a trail across Käringberget, east of Rörvattnet.

This path is difficult to follow at first, through forest and bogs, but on Käringberget you will probably be able to find cairns and follow those until you reach the end of the minor logging road, south of Överbäcken. This road descends towards the main road just south of the farm at Murunäset.

The gravel road then takes you into Gäddede. This is the same road that comes from Hällingsåfallet, should you decide to take the route from Valsjöbyn via Lobbersjön instead (2.15).

Gäddede is one of the bigger towns along The Green Ribbon. It has a good-sized store and a camping site with huts; they will probably hold a box for you. Gäddede is due to the rules of The Green Ribbon and the geography with the vast waters of Ströms Vattudal downstre-am, a place to which all hikers must come. The camping site is where Green Ribboners tend to congregate, including where NOBOs and SOBOs might meet and exchange stories and tips.

The routes north from Gäddede are described in Section 3.

139

Hiking is easy - you just keep on putting one foot in front of the other
until you are at Treriksröset.

KEEP ON

2.9 Helags – Vålådalen

Total distance: 42 km

Distances between waypoints:

⇨ Helags, mountain lodge

   11 km

⇨ Ljungan, rest hut

   12 km

⇨ Vålåstugan, overnight hut

   19 km

⇨ Vålådalen, mountain lodge

Effort: Medium. Mostly downhill with few climbs but a couple of fords that should be easy to medium.

Skills: Low. Well-marked trail with overnight huts and rest huts, tent not needed.

Summary: This is an excellent route, starting you off on Jämtland East. If you want to travel Jämtland West, you start with route 2.1. Once you reach Vålådalen, it becomes difficult to switch to Jämtland West. The Vålådalen and Ottsjö areas are very nice. You continue on routes 2.10 or 2.11 to Undersåker, which is a good place to resupply.

After an initial climb, the hiking is easy as you leave Helags Mountain Lodge behind and walk past some ponds and small lakes on the tundra at 900-1000 meters elevation. Passing the shoulder of Slaajve, you then descend slightly towards the river Ljungan and the rest hut. The soon-to-be impressive river is just a creek here, but there is no bridge, and you will have to ford. Usually, this is an easy ford.

From the hut, you climb steadily along the eastern rim of Härjångsfjällen and follow this until the trail descends to Härjångsån-Vålån. Fording this creek can be medium to difficult; it all depends (as always) on if it is early or late in the season and it has been raining heavily or not.

You are now close to Vålåstugorna, where a sparse growth of birch trees will greet you. The huts at Vålåstugorna are run by STF and have beds, a kitchen, and a host operating a small store during summer.

The shortest route to Vålådalen follows the mountainside north, with lovely views of the beautiful old-growth forest to the east, the Vålådalen Nature Reserve. The trail forks, the left trail leading to

Stensdalsstugorna and the right leading to Vålådalen. You are in the forest from now on, and a bridge will take you across Stensån and on to Vålådalen Mountain Lodge.

An alternative route from Helags to Vålådalen will be to take the trail from Helags to the Gåsen huts and then on to Stensdalsstugorna or Vålåstugorna. From there, you go to Vålådalen according to route 2.9.

From Vålåstugorna, there are also nice alternatives. One is taking the trail east to Lunndörrsstugan and then through some lovely old-growth forest down to Vålådalen. You can also leave the trail between Vålåstugorna and Lunndörrsstugan on the east side of the bridge across Tronnan-Vålån. You follow this big creek downstream through majestic pines and several small rapids to the fall, Vålåfallet. This is one of my favorite forest areas, From the fall a footpath will take you to Vålådalen Mountain Lodge.

This is a place with charming, old-style buildings and a fascinating sports history. Visionary Gösta Olander had new ideas on how athletes should train in the 1940s. A testimony to this training was his success with runner Gunder Hägg, who for a period held all ten world records for distances 1500-5000 m. Vålådalen was, for decades, a place where national team skiers and track and fielders used to train. Those days are gone, though.

At the Vålådalen lodge, you will find food, lodgings, and a small store for hikers. They will likely hold a box for you. For a bigger resupply, I recommend Undersåker, where there is a well-stocked grocery store, although the mountain lodge might be better stocked for freeze-dried food.

143

2.10 Vålådalen – Ottfjället – Undersåker

Total distance: 38 km

Distances between waypoints:

⇨ Vålådalen, mountain lodge

   13 km

⇨ Sörbotten, bridge

   11 km

⇨ Grofjällstugan, rest hut

   5 km

⇨ Small road

   7 km

⇨ Main road

   2 km

⇨ Undersåker, village

Effort: Medium to High. Several steep climbs and descents.

Skills: Low. Well-marked trails, rest huts available.

Summary: This is a lovely walk with fantastic views, an alternative to walking the road from Vålådalen to Undersåker. It is fairly demanding with many ups and downs, which is the price you pay for the views. This is the high route, in poor weather, you might want to pick the second option described in Vålådalen – Ottsjön – Undersåker (2.11).

From Vålådalen Mountain Lodge, you take the trail by the ski slope, leading to the top of Ottfjället. This is a steep climb but worth it. There are spectacular views all around. You see Helags and the other mountains from whence you came. Below you see lake Ottsjön and the steep descent you will take to Sörbottnen.

Leaving the bridge across Skårrån, you begin another climb up on Hållfjället and then down again before climbing to Grofjället. This is the last tundra mountain you will visit for a long time; on Jämtland East the forest will be your home until north of Valsjöbyn, some 150 kilometers of walking from here.

From Grofjällsstugan, you have several trails that will take you down to the minor road running south of and along the creek Henån. In good weather, you might prefer the path keeping you above the tree line and descending at Skavhuggen. Going straight down into the forest, past the rest hut, and following the road is probably more attractive in poor weather.

Once on that road, you follow it east until you hit the main road north to Undersåker and take it across the bridge and into the village. This road bridge is the only realistic crossing of the big river Indalsälven.

In Undersåker, you have a grocery store and lodgings that will probably hold a box for you. This is an excellent place to resupply if you do not want to go to the ski resort Åre. If you do this, you will have to backtrack to hit the 2. 12 route at Åre Björnen.

North of Undersåker/Åre the next place where you encounter a store is in Rötviken, around 130 kilometers along Jämtland East. Unless you have sent boxes to places in between, you will have to plan your food accordingly.

Many trails lead from Vålådalen.

2.11 Vålådalen – Ottsjön – Undersåker

Total distance: 32 km

Distances between waypoints:

⇨ Vålådalen, mountain lodge

  6 km

⇨ Vallbo Fjällgård, food and lodgings

  6 km

⇨ Ridvadet, lake ford, south side

  0,5 km

⇨ Ridvadet, lake ford, north side

  15 km

⇨ Small road

  2,5 km

⇨ Main road

  2 km

⇨ Undersåker, village

Effort: Low to Medium. Uphill to Ottsjö and the top of Välliste.

Skills: Low. Navigation easy, trails well maintained, rest huts available.

Summary: This is a nice walk given as an alternative to walking the road from Vålådalen to Undersåker. It has a spectacular ford across a lake.
This is the low route, in weather with good visibility you might want to pick the 2.10 route option, over the top of Ottfjället.

You follow the signposted trail (not the road) from Vålådalen to Vallbo. It goes south of the river. From Vallbo, you follow the path to where the map says "Ridvadet" on a promontory on the south side of lake Ottsjön. (WGS84 63.200583, 13.106472). If the weather is nice, a wonderful, sandy beach is made for a break and a bath.

The unique thing about this place is that you can walk in the water for about 500 meters, straight across the lake. Ridvadet ("The Riders' Ford") was used by cavalry or riders carrying mail hundreds of years ago before roads were built in this area.

The sandy beach continues into the water, and slightly below the lake's surface, there is a ridge you can walk upon, straight across to the northern shore. The ford is usually knee-deep, but that depends on how tall you are and the lake's level on that particular day.

It is quite an experience to walk across a lake like this. However, in high winds with waves, it can be dangerous. You will have to judge for yourself. If you decide against fording, you can follow the beach towards the southeast and walk on the road from Vålådalen to Undersåker. Boring, but a good emergency exit.

On the northern shore, you locate the trail that will take you uphill to Ottsjö village. There is a grocery store as well as lodgings.

Leaving Ottsjö, you take the trail towards, and straight across, the mountain Välliste. From the top, you have beautiful views in any direction. You see the mountains to the south where you came from and to the north the forests ahead. You will be walking in forests for some 150 kilometers, until north of Valsjöbyn, if you follow the Jämtland East route.

The trail continues north-westerly from Välliste, steeply down along Sågbäcken, and comes to a minor road. Take that road east until you reach the main road from Vålådalen and north to Undersåker and follow it across the bridge and into the village. This bridge is the only realistic crossing of the big river Indalsälven.

In Undersåker, you have a grocery store and lodging that will probably hold a box for you. This is an excellent place to resupply if you do not want to go to the ski resort Åre. If you do that, you will have to backtrack to hit the route at Åre Björnen. (2.12)

The next place where you encounter a store north of Undersåker/ Åre is in Rötviken, around 130 kilometers to the north. Unless you have sent boxes to places in between, you will have to plan your food accordingly.

Ford across Lake Ottsjön.

2.12 Undersåker – Vike/Olden

Total distance: 82 km

Distances between waypoints:

⇨ Undersåker, village

   11 km

⇨ Åre Björnen, ski center

   15 km

⇨ Bonäset, bridge

   9 km

⇨ Road to Nörder-Sandtjärnvallen

   8 km

⇨ Djuptjärnen, house

   19 km

⇨ Väg norrut, west of Höbodvallen

   20 km

⇨ Vike/Olden, logging road

Effort: Low. Almost all roads, some inclines.

Skills: Low to Medium. A couple of short parts of the route demand cross-country navigation in forests.

Summary: This route mostly follows roads and logging roads through the forest north towards Rötviken. It is based on what Ribboners call Svantes genväg (Svante's shortcut), and you might find detailed maps on the internet. In Vike/Olden, this route meets the one from Kolåsen (2.7), which is a connection between Jämtland East and West. In Rötviken, Jämtland East unites with Jämtland West when routes 2.5 and 2.13 meet.

From Undersåker, you follow the trail and signs for St Olavsleden. This is an old pilgrim trail from the east coast of Sweden to Trondheim and the tomb of St Olav on the coast of Norway.

About midway to Björnen, the trail will cross the highway, and after a while, you must leave the trail and recross the highway to where the serpentine road climbing to the ski center at Åre Björnen begins.

Björnen is the eastern end, at least for now, of the bustling and expanding ski resort of Åre. In Åre village you can find anything you want and more so. Restaurants, lodgings, sports shops, and grocery stores. The downside is that it is another 4 kilometers on St Olavsleden, and you have to backtrack to connect with route 2.12 at Björnen.

The route takes you from Björnen along the south shore of Fröå-tjärnen on minor roads and trails. The route passes Fröån, then turns north past Storflon. You take the path by Tjärntorpet and curve around the end of lake Stortjärnen. The trail then goes south and east to Ol-Olsvallen and reaches the essential road bridge at Bonäset.

From the bridge at Bonäset, you hike north on a reasonably busy hardtop road. After 9 kilometers, you take a tiny road going north to the house at Nörder-Sandtjärnvallen. You continue on another logging road north from this house until this road ends just southeast of the pond Djuptjärnen. You then make your way across country to the northwest for some 800 meters, down to Djuptjärnen and the house at its northern end.

From the house at Djuptjärnen, you walk north on roads past the houses at Djupsjö for 19 kilometers until you reach a logging road about 1 kilometer west of Höbodvallen (WGS84 63.597472, 13.585500).

You take this road almost, but not quite to its end. You then set your course more or less straight north, aiming for the logging road coming down from Rörtjärnen. The off-road distance is roughly 1300 meters. You find the road head here (WGS84 63.617778, 13.574972).

You follow this logging road north and east, past Västsjön to Björnnäset, where you turn north towards Vike och Olden. At Vike, you turn north on a logging road (WGS84 63.693778, 13.659333).

From this waypoint, the route is described under Vike/Olden – Rötviken (2.13). At Olden/Vike you also encounter the route from Kolåsen, connecting Jämtland West and Jämtland East. This route is described in the chapter Kolåsen – Vike/Olden (2.7).

Long term parking.

2.13 Vike/Olden – Rötviken

Total distance: 52 km

Distances between waypoints:

⇨ Olden/Vike, cross roads

   18 km

⇨ Jänsmässholmen, village

   11 km

⇨ Ansätten, farmhouse, locked

   23 km

⇨ Rötviken, village

Effort: Low. Mostly flat, a lot of road walking. Boggy and wet in places.

Skills: Low to Medium. Paths are not always easy to find.

Summary: This is a route mainly on small gravel roads through the forest. In Rötviken, there is a store for resupply, and Jämtland West connects through route 2.5 with Jämtland East.

At Vike, you turn north on a minor road (WGS84 63.693778, 13.659333). This route follows logging roads to slightly north of Håll-bodarna. At that place the road reaches and the route switches to an old, not well maintained winter trail. This will take you across what Green Ribboners like to dramatize as "The Bog from Hell." Wet and full of bugs in season. However, some say that it is not as bad as rumoured, and my guess is that it is hated most by hikers hoping to keep their feet dry and failing.

After the bog, the winter trail hits the road slightly south of Jäns-mässholmen. This is the kind of village with farmhouses scattered over a relatively wide area. There might be lodgings and people that will hold a box for you. When I was there on a rainy afternoon, the lodge looked very much closed. You must check on the internet.

From Jänsmässholmen you take the footpath leading north (marked with black dots on the map, the winter trail is wetter) towards the old farm Ansätten (WGS84 63.864972, 13.910139), not to be confused with Ansättenstugan. From Ansätten, you follow the path along Ansättsån until it reaches a road head and continue on that road. This road runs along the beautiful little river, and there are several lovely falls, one of which is Storforsen.

You can take a side trail that leads towards Rörvattnet, but I recommend continuing on the gravel road until it reaches a hardtop road 1 kilometer south of Rötviken. This is because Rötviken has a store for resupply and the gravel road is more affable and less trafficked than the hardtop road from Rörvattnet to Rötviken, which you will have to walk otherwise. However, Rörvattnet has an excellent camping site with a restaurant (serving bear burgers when I passed), and they will probably hold a box for you, so it is an option.

In Rötviken, there is also a camping site with huts and a well-stocked store, both of which might hold a box for you, but no restaurant.

In Rötviken Jämtland East meets Jämtland West, staying together until Valsjöbyn (2.14). Whether you travel Jämtland East or West, Rötviken is the first place with a grocery store for resupplies since Storlien or Undersåker/Åre. If you do not want to carry food for those entire stretches, you must send boxes ahead

This route has a lot of walking on gravel roads.

2.14 Rötviken – Valsjöbyn

Total distance: 17 km
Distances between waypoints:
⇨ Rötviken, village
   3 km
⇨ Hotagen, church
   6 km
⇨ Toskströmmen, bridge
   8 km
⇨ Valsjöbyn, village

Effort: Low. Hardtop road walking the entire distance.
Skills: Low. Road walking.

Summary: This is a dull bit of road walking but difficult to avoid. You need the road bridge to get across the chain of lakes at Toskströmmen. The setting is beautiful, though; you follow the water all the way. From Valsjöbyn, where there is a store and camping, two route suggestions will lead you to Gäddede. One is Jämtland West by Murfjället (2.8), with a lot of tundra mountains and some roads and Jämtland East with a lot of roads and some tundra mountains.

You take the road from Rötviken, passing the church at Hotagen and the bridge at Toskstömmen. North of Toskströmmen, there is information on an army installation called Klintaberg, built during World War II and used into the 1980s.

You can leave the hardtop road on paths before reaching Valsjöbyn if you plan to head for Vinklumpen and use the Lobbersjön route. This might be an option if you have already resupplied in Rötviken. The store in Valsjöbyn is well stocked for resupply. There is also a camping site a kilometer on the wrong side of the village (you have to backtrack). Both store and camping site might hold a box for you.

In Valsjöbyn, you have a choice between a westerly route, across Murfjället (2.8), which will take you to Gäddede with less road walking than the easterly route via Lobbersjön (2.15), which also is a bit longer.

The fall of Storforsen in river Ansättsån

2.15 Valsjösbyn – Lobbersjön – Gäddede

Total distance: 71 km

Distances between waypoints:

⇨ Valsjöbyn, village

   11 km

⇨ Vinklumpen, leave road

   20 km

⇨ Lobbersjön, Sami camp

   16 km

⇨ Hällingsåfallet

   16 km

⇨ Murunäset, farm

   8 km

⇨ Gäddede, village

Effort: Low. Some ascents. A lot of road walking.

Skills: Low. Lots of road walking and visible trails.

Summary: The Lobbersjön route is longer than the alternative by Murfjället (2.8) and has about 40 kilometers of road walking compared to 18 kilometers by Murfjället. The first half, before Hällingsåfallet, is nice. In Gäddede, there is lodging, a camping site, and a well-stocked store.

From Valsjöbyn, you follow roads and trails to Myrbodarna and the road to Vinklumpen Sami camp. The map shows a footpath as a dotted line (WGS84 64.100083, 14.341889) before you reach the Renslakteri, and you take this path north to the top of the tundra hill Vinklumpen. If you miss or lose this path, you aim for the top of Vinklumpen, and you will find the path sooner or later. It soon becomes a well-traveled quad trail that will take you across a nice tundra plateau towards Lobbersjön.

At Lobbersjön you will pass between several modern huts belonging to the Sami camp. They will be locked most of the time, but in summer, some families spend time there, usually in connection with gathering the reindeer.

More than ten years before my Green Ribbon hike, I walked through this area and found it an out-of-the-way location with little activity and some charming, ancient houses. Now the site is different, with quad tracks and recently built houses. Nothing remains the same, so writing a guidebook is a precarious business.

From Lobbersjön, you continue along the quad track to Muns-vattnet, where you take the trail going north and connecting to the logging road north of Stormyrhöjden and south of Fallhöjden. You follow this road and then pick the trail taking you across Hällingsån and Hällingsåfallet, on the bridge you see on the map. Hällingsåfallet is a waterfall worth a visit, and the bridge runs right on top of it. I walt-zed around in the forest looking for the bridge; if you miss the path, follow your ears to the fall. At the falls, the Hällingsån tumbles some 40 meters into a canyon that runs at right angles to the river, which is unusual with waterfalls.

From Hällingsåfallet, you walk some 22 kilometers on a gravel road into Gäddede. Before Murunäset, you pass the logging road where the route from Valsjöbyn via Murfjället connects (2.8).

Gäddede is a good-sized town with a good-sized store and a cam-ping site with huts, where Green Ribboners tend to congregate. The campsite will probably hold a box for you.

Gäddede is due to the rules of The Green Ribbon and the geo-graphy with the vast waters of Ströms Vattudal downstream, a place to which all Ribboners are channeled. The routes north will be described in Section 3.

Near Lobbersjön.

Flat hiking towards Lobbersjön.

Section 3: Gäddede – Hemavan

This is also an uncomplicated section. You will leave the region of Jämtland and enter Västerbotten. There are two alternative routes from Gäddede. These are 3.1 by Raukasjö and 3.2 by Sutme. Those routes converge at Slipsikstugan, near Klimpfjäll. The rest of the section to Hemavan will follow Lapplandsleden (3.3). This trail through a beautiful mountain area with deep valleys saw few visitors before the trail was established. Lapplandsleden goes from Borgafjäll to Hemavan where it ties on to Kungsleden. This will be described in Section 4, and and so will plenty of alternatives to Kungsleden. Section 3 is approximately 240-250 kilometers, depending on your choices.

he Lapland Trail near Raavrevarrtoe.

Dalavardo
Rävfallet
Tärnasjö
Røssvatnet
Sytertoppen
1 768 möh
Hemavan
Gränssjö
Marsfjället
1 590 m
Storuman
Klimpfjäll
Slipsikstugan
Raukasjö
Sutme
NORWAY
SWEDEN
Tunnsjøen
Gäddede
Murfjället
Lobbersjön
Grubbdalen
Valsjöbyn
Rötviken
Strömsund
Kallsjön
Olden
0
50 km
Åre
Undersåker
Storsjön
Östersund
3

3.1 Gäddede – Raukasjö – Klimpfjäll

Total distance: 101 km

Distances between waypoints:

⇨ Gäddede, village

  10 km

⇨ Lillfjället, rest hut

  18 km

⇨ Väktarmon, farm

  8 km

⇨ Baelkieabåårhke, rest hut

  6 km

⇨ Sielken, Sami camp (trail junction)

  5 km

⇨ Rödfjällsstugan, rest hut

  6 km

⇨ Ankarede, village

  11 km

⇨ Tjärnbäcken, rest hut

  14 km

⇨ Raukasjö, farm

  11 km

⇨ Slipsikstugan, overnight hut

  8 km

⇨ Saxån, bridge

  4 km

⇨ Klimpfjäll, village

Effort: Low to Medium. Some ascents.

Skills: Low. Well-marked trails most of the way. Tent needed.

Summary: This is an excellent route where you alternate between forest and tundra many times. It is an alternative to the route Gäddede - Sutme - Klimpfjäll (3.2) and is about 10 kilometers shorter. At Klimpfjäll you connect to Lapplandsleden (3.3) towards Hemavan.

The first kilometers are identical to the route from Gäddede via Sutme (3.2). You cross the river on the dam in midtown Gäddede and head for the ski slope at Brattliden. Soon a gravel road will take you towards the lift system, where you pick the summer trail running

Not always easy to see in which direction the arrows point.

Coffee at Slipsikstugan.

parallel to the road until you reach the fencing around the rengärde. You choose the summer trail going northeast, leading towards Lill-fjället and that rest hut.

The trail continues mostly through forest and some relatively dry marshland until you dip down into Väktarmon, an isolated farm at the road's end. The climb from the farm is pretty steep; the trail then dips and climbs again to the rest hut at Baelkieabåårhke.

In the valley below Baelkiesbåårhke, the trail passes the Sami summer camp of Sielken before heading up to the tundra on Röd-fjället and that rest hut.

It is downhill into the forest to Ankarede, a small village with an old church town worth visiting. A church town is a collection of old buildings used by nomadic Sami and farmers living far from churches. In earlier times, they could not travel to the church in a single day. Instead, the church towns were peopled on special weekends, when baptisms and weddings were performed. And, of course, a lot of partying. Today Ankarede Café is known for its waffles and might hold a box for you.

The trail follows Lejarälven northeast to the falls and then continues through forest and marshland to the Tjärnbäcken rest hut. After crossing the bridge at Raukaselet, you follow the road to Raukasjö, where the trail forks, and you take a right.

Heading northeast and after ascending, the trail will travel pleasantly across relatively flat marshland and tundra to Slipsikstugan. This is where you join the official trail Lapplandsleden. This is also where hikers will come using the route described in the chapter Gäddede - Sutme - Klimpfjäll (3.2).

Leaving Slipsikstugan, you walk across flat tundra, and then the trail dips down into the valley and the bridge over river Saxån. Descending, you pass some traditional Sami buildings and information about the Sami village that used to be there.

Most hikers will want to enter Klimpfjäll for resupply, which means 4 kilometers of road walking. If not, the trail continues on the north side of the hardtop road.

Klimpfjäll is a sizable village with several hotels and a store. These might hold a box for you. It is the last place to resupply before Hemavan unless you can send a box to Gränssjö. This is described in the chapter Klimpfjäll – Hemavan (3.3)

The tundra north of Raukasjö.

3.2 Gäddede – Sutme – Klimpfjäll

Total distance: 113 km

Distances between waypoints:

⇨ Gäddede, village

16 km

⇨ Sitejokkstugan, rest hut

10 km

⇨ Jougdaberg, farm

10 km

⇨ Blomhöjden, farm

18 km

⇨ Härbergsdalen, bridge

13 km

⇨ Värjaren, farm

16 km

⇨ Sutme, camping site with huts

8 km

⇨ Korpån, rest hut

10 km

⇨ Slipsikstugan, overnight hut

8 km

⇨ Saxån, bridge

4 km

⇨ Klimpfjäll, village

Effort: Medium. Several steep climbs.

Skills: Low to Medium. Trails are generally good, tent is needed.

Summary: This is an alternative to the Raukasjö route (3.1) from Gäddede, and it is about 10 kilometers longer, but with more spectacular scenery. The route connects with Lapplandsleden north of Sutme. Lapplandsleden is a trail that goes between Borgafjäll and Hemavan.

The first kilometers are identical to the route from Gäddede via Raukasjö, described in that chapter (3.1). You cross the river on the dam in midtown Gäddede and head for the ski slope at Brattliden. Soon a gravel road will take you towards the lift system, where you pick the summer trail running parallel to the road until you reach the fencing around the rengärde. You take the trail leading straight east, through the rengärde, towards the rest hut Sitejokkstugan.

At the old, abandoned farm Jougdaberg, you cross the valley Jougd-dalen, a wild, forested area that is a nature reserve. The trail climbs steeply to the tundra and then descends to the farms and houses around Blomhöjden. You walk a gravel road through the village and then pick up the trail heading northwest. The trail to the bridge at the western end of Gransjön is easy walking and beautiful. I especially remember the first time I walked it, on a lovely evening in early summer.

Another steep climb takes you to the tundra, and before heading down into Härbergsdalen, you have magnificent views up the valley and the impressive rockface of Mount Sielkentjahke. The area is sometimes called "the Sarek of Jämtland." Sarek is a spectacular national park that you will encounter further north, and Jämtland is the province and region you are in right now.

Another climb from Härbergsdalen to the tundra follows, and then the trail dips into the Daima valley. This is a wild nature reserve of forest and marshland. You can follow the valley and the winter trail and then take the road to Borgafjäll. There you will find a store, lodgings, and restaurants. Some will probably hold a box for you. This is the beginning, or end, of Lapplandsleden (the Lapland Trail) to Hemavan.

165

Bridge near Gransjön.

Härbergsdalen towards Sielkentjahke.

The walk along Daiman to Borgafjäll is very marshy, wet but wild; I have walked it a couple of times. However, I suggest you take a shortcut to Lapplandsleden via Sutme and bypass Borgafjäll.

The trail towards Sutme passes the abandoned farmstead of Värjaren and then climbs steeply to the tundra. From there, it gradually descends to the bridge across Sannarån. A road will take you to Sutme stugby, a private operation, where you can rent a cabin. They might hold a box for you.

Lapplandsleden was established 2021 and in this area replaces the old trail between Sutme and Slipsikstugan, so connecting to that newer trail is best. You walk from Sutme Stugby to the Sami summer camp of Sutme/Sodtme one kilometer up the valley. There you take the trail leading straight east, over a tundra pass, and connect to Lapplandsleden east of Tjaervietjålhte.

Heading north on Lapplandsleden, you will see the Korpån rest hut in the distance. From the rest hut, the trail climbs to the tundra. Part of the route is high indeed, with spectacular views, which also means some arduous and sometimes pointless ups and downs. It is also exposed to windy and rainy weather. The winter route and old trail to Slipsikstugan could then be an alternative.

You leave the high road and ascend to Slipsikstugan, where hikers using the route described in the chapter Gäddede – Raukasjö – Klimpfjäll (3.1) will arrive from another direction.

Leaving Slipsikstugan, you first cross flat tundra, and then the trail dips down into the valley and the bridge over river Saxån. Descending, you pass some traditional Sami buildings and information about the Sami village that used to be there.

Most hikers will want to enter Klimpfjäll for resupply, which means 4 kilometers of road walking. If not, the trail continues on the north side of the hardtop road.

Klimpfjäll is a sizable village with several hotels and a store. These might hold a box for you. It is the last place to resupply before Hemavan unless you can send a box to Gränssjö. This route is described in the chapter Klimpfjäll - Hemavan (3.3).

The rest hut at Korpån.

3.3 Klimpfjäll – Hemavan

Total distance: 141 km

Distances between waypoints:

⇨ Klimpfjäll, village

9 km

⇨ Durren, rest hut

10 km

⇨ Tjåkkelestugorna, overnight hut

17 km

⇨ Åtnikstugan, overnight hut

22 km

⇨ Gränssjö, camping site

26 km

⇨ Arevattnet, overnight hut

9 km

⇨ Daevne, rest hut

11 km

⇨ Atostugan, rest hut

37 km

⇨ Hemavan, village

Effort: Medium to High. There are quite a few steep ascents.

Skills: Low. The trail is well marked. There are huts and rest huts, but you need a tent.

Summary: You are on the official Lapland Trail from Klimpfjäll, connecting to Kungsleden in Hemavan (4.1). It is a very nice route through some beautiful mountains that few had traveled before Lapplandsleden was established in 2021.

From the village center in Klimpfjäll, you take the road and then the trail going up, passing under the ski lift. If you do not stop in the village, the trail from Slipsikstugan crosses the highway a couple of kilometers west of Klimpfjäll, close to the Saxån bridge. You will meet this trail north of Tjuthornsfjället.

Soon after leaving Klimpfjäll, you ascend to the tundra and hike past Durrenstugan, a rest hut at the mouth of the dramatic valley of Durrenskalet. After that valley and descending into birch forest, you come to Tjåkkelestugorna, a picturesque old farmstead that has become overnight huts. There is no host nor service at the time of writing. The regional administration, Västerbottens Länsstyrelse, manages all the huts along Lapplandsleden.

The trail continues along beautiful Remdalen, with very easy going for another 8 kilometers before it makes a turn east and climbs across the mountain of Raavrevarrtoe.

Dipping down into the valley of the creek Vojmån, you encounter another unmanned overnight hut at Åtnikstugan. The trail continues along the valley of Vojmån and follows the fence at Vardofjäll. Vardofjäll is a working farm and, as such, one of the few in Sweden without road access.

The trail ascends across Östra Vardofjället and then finds its way down into the forest to the hardtop road leading west into Gränssjö. In Gränssjö, there is a camping site with huts. They might hold a box for you.

From Gränssjö, you will now hike on the hardtop road towards Norway for about 8 kilometers. The Lapland Trail, signposted, then leaves the road and climbs very steeply to the top of Skaalmavaartoe. I came down that trail in the rain and wondered if it would be at all possible to mount it in the opposite direction. Improvements might have been made since.

Old trail, old sign, old bike in Remdalen.

The trail then follows the ridge of Skaalmavaartoe past Aamere. The views all around are marvelous, but the trail was not easy to follow in places, and there were some very steep, but short, passages. Your best bet is to walk where it looks easiest and use the trail more as an indication.

A steep descent into the valley west of lake Skalvattnet follows and then another very steep climb across the mountain of Stoere Tjåhke. This is one of the more challenging climbs you will encounter between Grövelsjön and Treriksröset, and the descent towards Arevattnet is just as steep.

At Arevattnet, you find an unmanned overnight hut from which the trail climbs again to the tundra and some nice and comfortable hiking north. After a relatively easy ford over Rigkerjohke about 10 kilometers later, you pass the rest hut at Daevne. I found that the winter trail was sometimes a better choice than the summer trail in this area. Less pointless ups and downs in many places. This is a perfect opportunity to practice off-trail skills and find a good line of hiking, using the trail more for reference. Walking on the tundra in the area is easy; no footpath is really needed.

The trail descends into the forest as you approach Atostugan. There are some interesting signposts about the old Sami way of living around that hut. The mountain of Atoklimpen is very special and has been sacred to the Sami for a long time. It consists of the extremely hard material peridotite, which has resisted erosion for several ice ages that have rolled over the mountain. The flora is also special, limited by the mineral content in the rocks.

Lapplandsleden follows the road north to Övre Jovattnet, and the Lapland Trail signs will guide you along the lake Kalven and then into the forest. Lapplandsleden is doing some strange twisting around in this area, from what I understand because landowners have not permitted a trail to be built otherwise. There is even a short stretch of water with rowboats in the lake Skälvattnet for this reason. My advice is to skip Lapplandsleden and make your own way between Joesjö at Övre Jovattnet and the old farm at Skälvattnet. As an individual, the law of common access gives you the right to walk wherever you please, except in someone's backyard. Also: skip the hassle with the boats and

Walking the wide ridge Skalmavaartoe.

find your way on land to where Lapplandsleden starts to climb away from the lake Skälvattnet.

From this lake, the trail ascends steeply through the forest and levels out on the tundra taking another dip again, before climbing to Rikarfjället.

This is the last bit of tundra walking before Hemavan; the trail will turn north and wind through the forest and around several small fishing lakes, some with lean-to shelters with fireplaces in front. Then it is downhill again, crossing the river Umeälven on a bridge and walking along the airstrip towards the center of town.

Hemavan is a good-sized place with restaurants, lodgings, groceries, and a sporting goods store where I picked up a pair of fleece gloves cheaply. They also sold freeze-dried food. There are plenty of businesses that will probably hold a box for you. Hemavan marks the end of the Lapland Trail and the beginning of Kungsleden. The route suggestions north will be described in Section 4.

Section 4:
Hemavan – Abisko/Tornehamn

Kungsleden, the most well-known hiking trail in the Swedish mountains, runs between Hemavan and Abisko. Many Green Ribboners prefer this route on their way to Treriksröset. Kungsleden does take you through some marvellous areas. My favourite part is the one north of Vakkotavare to Abisko. But in places, Kungsleden is not so great. And it bypasses areas that are just as good as the best parts of Kungsleden. If not better. I will try to entice you into some of those less traveled mountains.

Similar to Jämtland in Section 2, I offer you a Lapland West and a Lapland East. As with Jämtland, the west is wilder and, in my opinion, a more memorable hiking experience.

The approximate distance for Lapland West is 500 kilometers, depending on which of my suggested routes you pick. Lapland East is roughly 480 kilometers.

Lapland West has more off-trail travel, fords, and other factors that demand or develop better hiking skills than Lapland West. The amount of road walking is similar for both Lapland East and West.

In my description Lapland West and Lapland East have several areas where you can switch from one to the other, so you can certainly change your mind along the route. Or make your personal combination.

The part of Lapland West between Tärnasjöstugan and Staloluokta was one of the best parts of my entire Green Ribbon thru-hike. From Staloluokta I took route 4.9 through Sarek, to Kungsleden and Lapland East. I left Kungsleden at Alesjaure, and took the western route to Pålnostugan. (4.12 and 4.13).

If you are on Lapland East I would also advice you to include Sarek. You leave Kungsleden in Kvikkjokk (described briefly in 4.5) and take Padjelantaleden towards Staloluokta. You can leave that trail in several places and enter Sarek. One site, Duoddar, is mentioned in route 4.9.

Narvik
Pålnostugan
Katterjåkk
Tornehamn
Abisko
Unna Allakas
Alesjaure
Sälka
Kebnekaise 2111 m
Ritsem
Vakkotavare
Saltoluokta
Sarek 2089 m
Staloluokta
Sarek
Rinim
Stora Lulevatten
Duottar
Aktse
Kvikkjokk
Skalka
NORWAY
SWEDEN
Vuoggatjålme
Jäkkvik
Dalavardo
Hornavan
Rävfallet
...ertoppen 768 möh
Tärnasjö
Ammarnäs
Uddjaure
Hemavan
0   50 km
4

4.1 Hemavan - Tärnasjöstugorna

Total distance: 37 km

Distances between waypoints:

⇨ Hemavan, village

   1 km

⇨ Kungsleden, start

   10 km

⇨ Viterskalstugan, overnight hut

   6 km

⇨ Syterskalet, rest hut

   6 km

⇨ Syterstugan, overnight hut

   14 km

⇨ Tärnasjöstugan, overnight hut

Effort: Low to Medium. The climb out of Hemavan is a bit steep.

Skills: Low. The trail is well marked, with rest huts, overnight huts, and many hikers.

Summary: You are on Kungsleden. The hike through Syterskalet is spectacular, and so are the bridges across the end of Tärnasjön. At Tärnasjöstugan, you make your first choice between the routes I have collected under Lapland West (4.7) and those under Lapland East (4.2).

From Hemavan, you take the road leading uphill towards the Naturrum and the "Golden Globe," where the portal marking the beginning of Kungsleden is.

The trail then climbs diagonally across an area with ski lifts before leaving these steel skeletons behind and taking off above timberline towards a spectacular U-valley, Syterskalet. Soon you hike past Viterskalsstugan, an overnight hut. There is usually a host and a small store.

The valley of Syterskalet is beautiful but also a funnel for winds. On the first night of a long hike with a homemade tent years ago, the wind had the rain flapping so vigorously that I could not sleep. I went out and pitched it anew, with the foot end towards the wind. This did not help, so I broke camp at 2 o'clock in the night and hiked for several hours against the wind and rain towards the rest hut, where I slept for an hour or two. Later, in Vuoggatjålme, I borrowed some tools and fixed the attachment of the hiking poles inside the tent. After that, I had no more problems.

The rest hut mentioned is situated between the mighty gateway walls of Syterskalet, and after that the country opens up. It is downhill to the overnight hut Syterstugan, managed by STF. There is a host and a small store.

When you reach lake Tärnasjön, there are several beautiful bridges between small islands, taking you across the lake's southern end. They have sometimes been nicknamed "The Golden Gate Bridges."

If the weather makes you feel like a bath, do it close to the bridges on some lovely, sandy beaches. The lake will soon disappear out of sight, even if the trail follows it to Tärnasjöstugan. STF runs it, and there is usually a host and a small store.

At Tärnasjöstugan, you make your first choice between Lapland East and West. If you go north towards Skidbäcksstugan, you are on Lapland West. This route is described in the chapter Tärnasjöstugan - Vuoggatjålme (4.7). If you continue Kungsleden going east, you are on Lapland East, the route described in Tärnasjöstugan – Ammarnäs (4.2).

"The Golden Gate bridges"

4.2 Tärnasjöstugorna – Ammarnäs

Total distance: 40 km

Distances between waypoints:

⇨ Tärnasjöstugan, overnight hut

   13 km

⇨ Servestugan, overnight hut

   7 km

⇨ Vuomatjåhkka, rest hut

   5 km

⇨ Juovvatjåhkka, rest hut

   8 km

⇨ Aigertstugan, overnight hut

   7 km

⇨ Ammarnäs, village

Effort: Low to Medium.

Skills: Low. Well-marked trail with plenty of overnight huts and rest huts available, tent not needed. Lots of hikers.

Summary: This part of Kungsleden takes you across the mountains to the village of Ammarnäs where there is road access. Overnight huts are run by STF, with hosts and a small store. Route 4.3 continues to Jäkkvik; you can also switch to Lapland West (4.7).

From Tärnasjöstugan, Kungsleden at first climbs steadily out of the forest to the tundra. It then dips down and crosses a bridge at Servestugan. Another bridge and a steep climb take you above the timberline to the rest hut at Vuomatjåhkka, which is on the winter trail, not the summer trail.

Fairly soon, you reach the rest hut at Juovvatjåhkka, but first, you have a steep ascent and then a descent over Juhtatvaratje. The trail meanders around lakes and small mounds before heading down rather steeply towards Aigertstugan, situated at the treeline with fine views of Ammarnäs and the lake Gautsträsket.

Another steep descent through the forest takes you to a road and then into Ammarnäs. There are regular buses to and from Ammarnäs, as well as restaurants, lodgings, and a grocery store. Some will likely hold a box for you.

Lake Tärnasjön.

4.3 Ammarnäs – Jäkkvik

Total distance: 91 km

Distances between waypoints:

⇨ Ammarnäs, village

   22 km

⇨ Rävfallsstugan, rest hut

   25 km

⇨ Sjnultje, rest hut

   15 km

⇨ Bäverholmen, food and lodgings (boat transport to Adolfström available)

   8 km

⇨ Adolfström, lodgings and small store, road access

   13 km

⇨ Pieljekaisestugan, rest hut

   8 km

⇨ Jäkkvik, village

Effort: Medium. Some pretty steep climbs. Some rocky terrain.

Skills: Low. Well-marked trail. Some huts.

Summary: This is a less-traveled part of Kungsleden than 4.2. The huts along this route have no hosts. Rävfallsstugan has locked overnight rooms, key available at Ammarnäs, Bäverholmen, and Adolfström. Pieljekaisestugan also has locked overnight rooms, keys available at Jäkkvik and Adolfström. At Rävfallsstugan and Laisälven, you can connect to Lapland West (4.7).

You start by climbing steeply out of Ammarnäs and following a tundra ridge with lovely views of Vindelälven, to which you descend and cross at Rävfallsstugan.

At this point, you can choose to take a lovely trail upstream along the river Vindelälven to Dalavardo. At Dalavardo, you are on Lapland West and can follow the wild side route described in the chapter Tärnasjöstugan to Vuoggatjålme (4.7).

Soon after Rävfallsstugan, you come to one of the steeper climbs on Kungsleden. Or at least that is how I remember it; a rainstorm hit when I was on it, which might have made it seem especially steep. You have now entered the administrative region of Norrbotten, although

Looking up the valley of river Vindelälven.

you are still in the province of Lapland, and this region manages many overnight huts and rescue huts. The remainder of The Green Ribbon hike will be in Norrbotten, which is enormous, covering about 20 percent of Sweden. This means it is bigger than Hungary and more than twice the size of Switzerland but with only 250 000 inhabitants.

The tundra continues past the rest hut at Sjnultje, the trail then descends into the valley of the impressive river Laisälven, which you cross on a bridge. At this point, you can leave Kungsleden and follow Laisälven upstream. I have fond memories of the rest hut at Kattugglekojan from a sunny evening in early summer. There is a path to start with, but this alternative soon involves quite a bit of off-trail hiking.

When you reach Hurasjåhkå, a major tributary to Laisälven, you can follow it upstream or ford it. If it is fordable (it was not when I was there), you can continue to Laisstugan and connect with Lapland West and the route described in the chapter Tärnasjöstugan to Vuoggatjålme (4.7). If you decide not to ford, you can follow Hurasjåhkå upstream through very aggressive junipers until you reach the bridge over Dadtjajåhkå. From that bridge, you travel northwest and connect to the trail leading to the Ruonekjåhkå rest hut, also on 4.7.

However, if you decide to stay on Kungsleden after the Laisälven bridge, you will come to the inn Bäverholmen, situated far from the nearest road. At Bäverholmen, you can get food and lodgings. They will likely hold a box for you, but Adolfström and Jäkkvik are probably better for that. You can also hire a boat ride from Bäverholmen to Adolfström; just make sure this is according to The Green Ribbon rules at the time of your hike.

The hiking trail continues to Adolfström, an old village with a fascinating history. This goes back to the mining operations around Nasafjäll and the late 1700s when a melter was built to process the ore, and the place for this was named Adolfström. A sawmill, a smithy, and dams are examples of what was built. Still, the mining operations were never profitable and ended around 1810. In 1821 many of the buildings were destroyed in a fire.

Today there are lodgings and a café in Adolfström, as well as road access. You can buy basic foodstuff and other things in the old, traditional, general store ("Handelsboden").

From Adolfström, the trail ascends slowly and then a bit more steeply towards the rest hut Pieljekajsestugan. Overnight rooms are available if you pick up a key in Adolfström, but part of the hut is open. You are in Pieljekaise National Park, this status is due to its beautiful, untouched birch forest.

You have fine views from the ridge above the hut in many directions before the trail descends steeply towards Jäkkvik. In Jäkkvik, there is road access with regular buses, a well-stocked store, restaurants, and lodgings. Several of these businesses might hold a box for you.

Traditional Sami sod goahti.

4.4 Jäkkvik – Kvikkjokk

Total distance: 80 km + 8 km boat
transport

Distances between waypoints:

⇨ Jäkkvik, village

   17 km + 5 km boat

⇨ Vuonatjviken, overnight hut

   21 km

⇨ Tjäurakåtan, rest hut

   9 km

⇨ Luspevaratj, bridge

   21 km

⇨ Tsielekjåkkstugan, rest/overnight
   hut

   12 km

⇨ Mallenjarka

   3 km boat

⇨ Kvikkjokk, village

Effort: Medium.

Skills: Low to Medium. Navigation is mostly easy; few huts, tent needed.

Summary: This is the wildest and least developed part of Kungsleden. Coming from the south, boat transport across lake Riebnes must be ordered in Jäkkvik. At Mallenjarka on the southern bank, you can telephone Kvikkjokk, although this might not work for all cell phone operators. Kvikkjokk has lodgings, store, and road access. You can connect to Lapland West.

This is an interesting part of Kungsleden because it is not as predictable as some others. Boat transports are one part of this; another is a scarcity of infrastructure, particularly overnight huts. This is the only part of Kungsleden where a tent is needed, probably explaining why many people do not travel it. For some people, like my son, when he thru-hiked Kungsleden, this is more of an advantage.

Starting from Jäkkvik, you walk across a dam, and soon reach a rest hut at the eastern part of lake Hornavan, Tjärvekallegiehtje, and a boat crossing. With luck, there are two rowboats on your side.

In that case, you row across and leave two boats on the other side. With my luck, there is usually only one boat to start with. In that case, you row across, pick up another boat and tow it back. Then, for the

Crossing with row boats.

third time, you row across the waters. There MUST always be at least one boat on each side.

The next lake to cross is Riebnes. There are no rowboats; you must order this transport with the people living in Vuonatjviken when you are in Jäkkvik. Vuonatjviken has huts with a self-service kitchen to offer.

Just north of Vuonatjviken, you pass through an area with giant pines. My favorite kind of forest. Soon after, you cross the Arctic Circle into The Land of The Midnight Sun. That is, if you are there on Midsummer's Eve, the sun does not set. The further north you get, the longer the period with Midnight Sun. At Treriksröset, the sun does not set at all between May 20 and July 20.

By the steamboat jetty in Jäkkvik.

The trail goes steeply down through dense vegetation towards lake Tjeggelvas and the bridges across the rapids at Luspevaratj. Then you ascend into open country. The expansive views from the slope of Goabddabakte disappear as you descend into the canyon of Suonje-gårsså, and soon you are at Tsielekjåkkstugan. This is a rest hut, but you can spend the night there since it is the only hut in the area. There is a stove, but no firewood, so you should pick up deadwood along the trail if you want a fire.

From Tsielekjåkkstugan, you travel across a park-like tundra plateau that reminded me of an African savanna the first time I saw the area. Then the trail dips steeply down into some old-growth forest towards Mallenjarka, where you need another boat taxi to take you across to Kvikkjokk. If your cell phone works (check with locals for cell phone companies), you can call a number usually posted on the south shore. There might be a timetable. Another, perhaps safer, means of contact for the boat taxi might be to use the emergency phone in Tsielekjåkkstugan. This is not considered an incorrect use of it.

Just so you know, you are on Kungsleden. Kvikkjokk Mountain Lodge.

185

Kvikkjokk has several alternative lodgings, including a store and a restaurant at the Kvikkjokk Mountain Lodge. There is road access and buses to Jokkmokk, a sizable town 120 kilometers away, where you will find almost everything you might need.

From Kvikkjokk, you can continue Kungsleden, route 4.5. In that description is also mentioned how you can take Padjelantaleden towards Staloluokta. That gives you the option to enter Sarek. This is also mentioned coming from Staloluokta in route description 4.9. Padjelantaleden from Kvikkjokk also lets you connect to Lapland West in Staloluokta and continue to Ritsem (4.10).

4.5 Kvikkjokk – Saltoluokta

Total distance: 65 km + 7 km boat transport

Distances between waypoints:

⇨ Kvikkjokk, village

16 km

⇨ Pårtestugan, overnight hut

19 km

⇨ Laitaure, rest hut

3 km boat transport or rowing, 1 km walking

⇨ Aktse, overnight hut

9 km

⇨ Svijnne, rest hut

4 km boat transport

⇨ Sitojaurestugorna, overnight hut

11 km

⇨ Ausutsjvagge, rest hut

9 km

⇨ Saltoluokta, mountain lodge

Effort: Medium. Some steep climbs.
Skills: Low. Well-marked, well-traveled trail. Huts and rest huts. Tent recommended.

Summary: South of Aktse, there is mostly forest, north there is mostly tundra. The trail runs close to the border of Sarek National Park, a jewel in the Swedish mountains. From Kvikkjokk and Aktse you can enter Sarek. Saltoluokta is a charming mountain lodge with a store and lodgings. Regular boat transport from the lodge to the road across the lake. You will probably have to walk a lot on that road for the official Green Ribbon, to Vakkotavare. If not, you take the bus.

Several alternative routes from Kvikkjokk are, in my opinion, much more attractive than Kungsleden. Some start by taking Padjelantaleden towards Staloluokta.

This trail, following the lush valley of Tarradalen, is more pleasant than following Kungsleden north to Aktse. On your way to the tundra, you walk in a beautiful birch forest abundant with flowers in many places. The forest will gradually peter out, a perfect way of entering the mountains. When you reach the huts at Duottar, you can leave the trail and travel cross country into Sarek National Park. The park is a highlight in the Swedish mountains and should not be missed. This alternative route is described in the chapter Staloluokta – Sarek – Aktse or Sitojaure (4.9).

If you continue Padjelantaleden, you can follow this trail past Staloluokta towards Ritsem, described in route 4.10.

However, now we leave Kvikkjokk on Kungsleden, and it initially ascends rather steeply through the evergreen forest. Coming up to the Dahta lakes, there is another way into Sarek, across Boarek. From the lakes, it is then reasonably level hiking on Kungsleden to Pårtestugan. You then climb briefly to the tundra before the trail drops down into the forest to the Laitaure rest hut. You find rowboats, the standard three with at least one to be left on each shore of the substantial lake Lajtavrre. Once in the fall, I waited for several hours for better visibility but finally lost patience and rowed across this lake in a fog, which was an interesting experience.

This was late in the fall; in summer there is a regular boat taxi service; you have to check the timetable. You cannot rely on cell phone reception from the southern shore. It is being discussed to re-route Kungsleden farther west, towards the boundary of Sarek, and build a bridge across the river Rahpaädno to avoid this lake crossing.

At Aktse, you have an overnight hut and a small store operated by the host. Aktse is probably the most beautifully situated of all farms established far into the mountains in the late 1800s or early 1900s. Another example of this is Vuoggatjålme.

Aktse is located at "The Gate of Sarek," You can travel by boat to the park boundary below the cube-shaped mountain Nammasj and then hike into the park on an unmarked but well-defined trail. This boat landing below Nammasj is also where you exit if you have chosen to walk down the Rapa valley, described in the chapter Staloluokta – Sarek – Aktse or Sitojaure (4.9).

Kungsleden climbs steeply north from Aktse. At the tree line, there is a path going west, leading to the top of Skierffe, the mountain with the sheer rock face that dominates the view at Aktse. The view from the top of Skierffe, with the multicolored pools of the delta below and the mighty peaks of Sarek to the west, has few rivals in the Swedish mountains. It is absolutely a recommended detour from Kungsleden. You can descend Skierffe towards the west and make

Langas hydropower dam.

your way to the boat landing below Nammasj, at the park boundary, and then hike into the Rapa Valley.

But we continue on Kungsleden, and after the steep climb from Aktse, this trail crosses a tundra mountain and then heads down, and pretty soon, you are at Svijnne. There is a rest hut and a boat taxi that you usually must book by phone from Aktse. It might also be running on a schedule. Do not expect cell phone coverage at Svijnne.

The boat takes you to Sitojaurestugorna, overnight huts with a host and a small store. The trail continues north with easy walking. There is a rest hut at Avtsusjvavgge, and soon after, you top out above the vast hydropower dam system, with great views despite the sadness surrounding it.

Every time I admire that expanse before descending to Saltoluokta Mountain Lodge, I wish I had seen that view a hundred years ago. When Langas below was a lake and not a hydropower dam. When Stora Sjöfallet (The Great Lake Fall) at its northern end was still cascading freely, considered to be one of the most magnificent in Europe. The area was made one of Sweden's and Europe's first national parks in

1909, with the explicit purpose of preserving the splendor of the fall. Which turned out not to mean much.

In 1919, the Swedish parliament decided to begin a process of hydro-power exploitation that would last more than four decades and leave just about nothing of the once-mighty falls. When a road was needed, it was expediently decided that a 100 meters wide strip straight through the park was no longer a National Park, and the road was then built.

What remains is the great mockery, despite all the ravaging, of still calling it both Stora Sjöfallet as well as a National Park.

Saltoluokta, down by the dam, is my favorite lodge in the Swedish mountains. It has managed to keep a rustic feeling from 1920 coupled with modern annexes with nice rooms and self-service kitchens. STF manages it, and there is a store and a restaurant. Across the lake, served by a regular boat taxi, you find the aforementiones road with buses running daily during summer. If you are officially on The Green Ribbon, the most common option is to walk this road to Vakkotavare. People "only" thru-hiking Kungsleden usually take the bus. See route description 4.6 for more on this.

4.6 Saltoluokta – Abisko

Total distance: 135 km

Distances between waypoints:

⇨ Saltoluokta, mountain lodge

30 km + 2 km by boat

⇨ Vakkotavare, overnight hut

14 km + 1 km by boat

⇨ Teusajaurestugorna, overnight hut

9 km

⇨ Kaitumjaurestugorna, overnight hut

6 km

⇨ Singistugorna, overnight hut

12 km

⇨ Sälkastugorna, overnight hut

9 km

⇨ Tjäktjapasset, rest hut

4 km

⇨ Tjäktjastugan, overnight hut

13 km

⇨ Alesjaurestugan, overnight hut

21 km

⇨ Abiskojaurestugan, overnight hut

14 km

⇨ Abisko Turist, mountain lodge

Effort: Medium to High. Several steep climbs.

Skills: Low. The trail is well marked, with rest huts, overnight huts, and has lots of hikers.

Summary: You are on Kungsleden and perhaps on the most spectacular part of that long trail. The part of the path passing Singi/Sälka, where many hikers come from Nikkaluokta and Kebnekaise, and north to Abisko is the most traveled mountain trail in Sweden. From Abisko, you have several alternative routes to Treriksröset, described in Section 5.

A boat runs several times daily across the lake Langas from Saloluokta to Kebnats and the road on the north shore. There is also a bus running daily from Gällivare to Ritsem and back during the peak of the summer, and if you hike Kungsleden, you typically will take this bus to the Vakkotavare hut. However, if you are officially on The Green Ribbon, you cannot take the bus from Kebnats, which means about 30

Evening in Saltoluokta

kilometers of road walking. An alternative is not to take the boat across to Kebnats but to backtrack up the incline from Salto. It might also be possible to follow the shore of Langas west from Saltoluokta to the dam at Suorva, but I have not found any reliable account of a route like that.

If you decide to backtrack to the top of the incline (you can of course skip going down to Saltoluokta in the first place), you follow the signs and trails leading towards Bietsavrre, and you walk along the south shore of that lake. Staying high to avoid willow shrubs is a good idea as you travel towards the distinctive mountain Slugga. You travel north to find the trail leading towards the dams at Jiertasuoloj and Suorva. Crossing the dams, you only have 9 kilometers of road walking to Vakkotavare.

If you walk the road from Kebnats, you might stop at the restaurant in Vietas for ice cream and a cup of coffee.

Once you get to Vakkotavare, there will be no more roads until Abisko, and to celebrate this, you start from the hut with one of the

Kungsleden north of Kaitumjaure.

steepest climbs on Kungsleden. Unfortunately, you lose a lot of this elevation rather quickly as you approach Teusajaure, where you find rowboats to bring you across. You can also signal for a boat taxi from the huts, where you have lodgings, a host, and a small store.

Yet another steep climb takes you up the hill towards Kaitum-jaurestugorna. After the climb it is easy hiking. The huts at Kaitum-jaure also have lodgings, a host, and a small store.

Before reaching Singistugorna, you can take a side trail east towards Kebnekaise Fjällstation. This has become a ritzy mountain lodge, with helicopters buzzing people in to climb Mount Kebnekaise, the highest peak in Sweden. The whole area north of the lodge is very very alpine with glaciers and popular among climbers.

Singistugorna is a relatively small place with lodgings, a host, and a small store. Sälkastugorna to the north gets more traffic and is a much bigger operation, with several hosts. The trail from Nikkaluokta and Kebnekaise Fjällstation to Sälka and Abisko is the most frequented hiking trail in the Swedish mountains.

Tjäktjavagge, looking south from Tjäktjapasset.

Halfway between Singi and Sälka, the Nordkalottleden joins from the west. This route is described in the section Ritsem – Hukejaure – Sälka (4.11).

There are exciting and spectacular route options from Sälka as an alternative to Kungsleden. You can take the trail to Nallostugan and continue to Vistasstugan. From there, you also have several options. One is to go north and connect to Kungsleden via Unna Visttasvaggi or Visttasvaggi. Another seldom traveled, spectacular and arduous route goes from Vistasstugan to Mårmastugan. You can reconnect with Kungsleden west of the lake Ahpparjavri or hike through the much-photographed (from the north) valley of Lapporten (The Lap Gate) down to Abisko.

If you stay on Kungsleden north of Sälka, you will soon climb to the highest elevation on the entire trail, Tjäktapasset, with a rest hut on top. Descending on the north side through rocky terrain and with lots of boardwalks, you pass Tjäktjastugan. This is a hut with lodgings, a host, and a small store.

The rest hut at Tjäktjapasset.

It is flat, easy walking to Alesjaurestugorna, which you see from afar. The buildings are situated on top of a hill, with the beautiful lake Alisjavri at its feet. There are lodgings, a host, and a small store. Not to mention a sauna.

From Alesjaure, you can connect to Lapland West, a route described in the chapter Alesjaure – Unna Allakas - Katterjåkk (4.12). If not, you follow Kungsleden along the lakes and then descend steeply into the valley with Abisko National Park. Tenting in the park is only allowed around Abiskojaurestugorna, and you must pay a fee for that. There are lodgings, a host, and a small store. One option is to set up camp high on the hillside before entering the park and then hike the following day to Abisko Turist, some 17–18 kilometers.

When you get to Abisko, you have reached the end, or the beginning, of Kungsleden. Do not confuse Abisko Turist, run by STF, with Abisko Mountain Lodge situated a couple of kilometers away, near Abisko Östra. Both places have lodgings and restaurants and will probably hold a box for you.

Abisko and "The Lap Gate".

Abisko Turist is a big lodge and hostel with a sizable store, self-service kitchens, and standard hotel rooms. There is a nice restaurant with views of the vast lake Torneträsk. Situated nearby is a nature interpretation center that is well worth a visit. There is both road and rail access in Abisko.

Should you wish for a well-stocked supermarket, you must walk a couple of kilometers east to Abisko Östra. This could be done on your way to Torneträsk Station if you plan to take a boat taxi. This boat option is described in Abisko – Kattuvuoma – Vuoskojaure (5.2).

4.7 Tärnasjöstugan – Vuoggatjålme

Total distance: 104 km

Distances between waypoints:

⇨ Tärnasjöstugan, overnight hut

   13 km

⇨ Skidbäcksstugan, overnight hut

   14 km

⇨ Dalavardo, overnight hut

   13 km

⇨ Vindelkroken, bridge

   30 km

⇨ Laisstugan, overnight hut

   20 km

⇨ Ruonekjåhkå, rest hut

   14 km

⇨ Vuoggatjålme, lodge

Effort: Low to Medium. Some climbs and bogs.

Skills: Medium to High. The trail is not always well marked; cross-country navigation is needed. Few people, but some huts and rest huts.

Summary: This is Lapland West and another favorite route of mine. The scenery is perhaps not as dramatic as on some other routes, but you experience a walk through wild country, where few hikers go. From Dalavardo you can connect to Kungsleden on Lapland East at Rävfallsstugan (4.3). There are several opportunities to resupply near Vuoggatjålme.

Going north from Tärnasjöstugan quickly takes you into a country where you might hike for many days without seeing anyone.

The trail is easy to follow and easy to walk at the beginning, taking you up towards the tundra and then down again to Skidbäcksstugan. This used to be a small, old hut with a romantically smoke-darkened interior in a wilderness setting. The last time I passed, a new building with lots of glass was being built, with quad tracks used for transport running through the area. Change is inevitable, I guess, but my experience was definitely diminished. However, after another ten years of being "romantic" since my first visit, the old hut was probably ready for a remake. Skidbäcksstugan and several other huts are owned and managed by the regional administration in Västerbotten. These cabins do seldom have any host or store. You pay for the overnight huts by sending money according to instructions in the huts (or on the web).

From Skidbäcksstugan, you follow the summer trail up the hillside of Nassa and then down across some pretty boggy and wet country most of the way to Dalavardo. This is another overnight hut run by the region.

At Dalavardo, you can follow a lovely trail downstream along the river Vindelälven. This is one of four Swedish "national rivers," meaning that they are the only ones left being (almost) untouched by hydropower installations. This trail takes you to Kungsleden and Lapland East at Rävfallsstugan (4.3).

Lapland West continues north, upstream, along the trail to the Sami camp at Vindelkroken ("the Vindel hook"). The place is named after the 90-degree turn the river makes at that point. Vindelkroken is one of the nicest and best kept Sami summer camps I have encountered. There are several well-kept traditional Sami buildings along the trail. Count on them being empty and locked.

From Vindelkroken, you leave the trail for several days of glorious and pretty easy hiking across some tundra mountains. After the bridge across Vindelälven, keep to the path going uphill towards the rengärden shown on the map. Once you are above the willows, you take a right and leave the trail at about 700-800 meters of elevation. You stay on this elevation going east and around the mountain Gåbråjvvie.

You stay more or less on this elevation going northeast until you are straight east of Miehtjietjåhkka. There you cross the creek and head up the valley going northeast, which takes you to lake Tsaggiekjavrieh.

Following that lake and its neighbor on their eastern shores, you then travel down the southern slope of the mountain Alddatjåhkka. You cannot be sure to find the trail leading towards the bridge across Laisälven, but that bridge is your goal. Right after there is another bridge across a tributary, and then you are at Laisstugan. This is a gathering of houses for different purposes, some of them locked. Laisstugan is another unmanned, overnight hut managed by the region.

A possible route takes you upstream from Kungsleden along Laisälven to this hut, which I briefly mentioned in the section Ammarnäs – Jäkkvik (4.3).

You are back on a trail again, although it is difficult to find it in the dense brush near Laisstugan. You climb north and use the summer trail up on the tundra and into a wide basin where you will find a bridge. This is a so-called "summer bridge" because they are airlifted into place once the worst spring flood is over. If you hike very early in the season, you must check if such bridges are in place. The regional websites will have information on this.

The trail climbs towards a saddle from the bridge, then heads down again. At one point, the trail splits. You must not follow the apparent cairns leading right towards Suoddas. I made this mistake in a fog years ago, and it took me some time to get my bearings and get back on track. Take the left-hand trail heading for the forest and another bridge, next to the rest hut at Ruonekjåhkå.

Now you travel east, downstream this beautiful river. The path is mostly good, with many boardwalks taking you to the nice rapids, where the river empties into the lake Sädvvajavrre.

The trail continues and hits the highway just north of a road bridge. You walk on hardtop roads a few kilometers to Vuoggatjålme, where there is food and lodgings. They have no store, but they might help you with shopping and will likely hold a box for you if you stay there.

Nearby, Camp Polcirkeln has a small store, but the food was not very suitable for hikers on my visit. More suited for people in campers with microwave ovens. Another store lies north of where the trail from Ruonekjåhkå hits the hardtop, at Sandviken. They have a camping site with huts and a small store. They will probably pick you up by car where you reach the road and drive you back to the same place if you stay with them overnight. They will likely hold a box for you.

At any rate, you must walk past Vuoggatjålme to hike the magnificent Seldutdalen/Seldutvagge. Vuoggatjålme is another classic place in the Swedish mountains, once established as a farm with no road, a long way from anywhere. It is in a stunning location, between a big lake and a small lake. In winter, it often tops the list of the coldest place in Sweden. Today it is an elegant hotel with classy food, still run by descendants of the original settlers. They have several helicopters running out of their backyard, primarily for anglers and, in winter, skiers.

Coffee break near Miehtjietjåhkka.

The rapids in Ruonekjåhkå.

4.8 Vuoggatjålme – Staloluokta

Total distance: 115 km

Distances between waypoints:

⇨ Vuoggatjålme, lodge

27 km

⇨ Jurunvaratj, rest hut

11 km

⇨ Ikesjaure, rest hut

11 km

⇨ Mavasjaure, semaphore, south shore

2 km boat

⇨ Mavasjaure, north shore

23 km

⇨ Lajrrojåhkå, bridge

29 km

⇨ Staddajåkkstugan, overnight hut

12 km

⇨ Staloluokta, overnight hut

Effort: Low to Medium. Some climbs and bogs.

Skills: Medium to High. The trail is not always easy to follow. Few people, but some huts and rest huts. A couple of fords, some of the medium to high difficulty.

Summary: The beautiful valley Seldutdalen, north of Vuoggatjålme, is worth hiking. The last time I walked it, the trail was very poorly maintained. Ikesjaure and Mavasjaure are both beautiful lakes. The walk along Pieskehaure, with Mount Sulitelma ahead of you is more than spectacular if the skies are clear. You can connect to Kungsleden and Lapland East using Nordkalottleden from Pieskehaure to Kvikkjokk. From Staloluokta, you have many route alternatives.

You will be going straight north into Seldutvagge from Vuoggatjålme. This is one of the most beautiful birch wood valleys in the mountains. Few people, no huts, lots of lovely creeks tumbling down the mountainsides on your right

The last time I walked it, the trail was lousy, probably not having been maintained for 20 years. It took some GPS work to reconnect to the path when I lost it. Hopefully, the trail will be repaired; it is a beautiful hike through a valley that is relatively untouched by the modern world.

Coming up out of the valley to the tundra, a rest hut is located south of Jurunvaratj. The trail climbs to Ikesjaure, a spectacular lake with impressive rock faces on both shores. Local myth says a crashed airplane with valuables on board lies deeply under it's surface. Towards the eastern end of the lake, a sandy beach is suitable for swimming on a sunny day. So far, I have yet to experience a sunny day on Ikesjaure, though.

The trail climbs after the rest hut and takes you through a pleasant tundra valley. Then it is downhill into the forest to the lake Mavasjaure. The trail winds through the birch forest to the Semafor. There is also a grubby three-wall shelter with a fireplace in front.

The Semafor/semaphore is used to signal to the Sami camp on the northern shore that you would like a boat to pick you up. You turn the white side of the semaphore towards the lake. Sometimes they are so fast to launch a boat from the other side that you do not have time to make a cup of coffee; at other times, they are not so fast.

The boat ride is not a scheduled service, so it depends if anybody is at home, watching, and in the mood. When you see a boat coming

Old farm in Seldutvagge.

your way, you turn the semaphore back to neutral. You should check in advance to get a rough idea of the cost of the boat ride. And it is a cash business.

The trail goes between the houses on the northern shore, straight into the birch forest. After you have passed the small lake Bierre, it ascends to the tundra, and you have a glorious 15-kilometer hike waiting for you.

The vast lake Pieskehaure will be on your right, and for a long time, you will be walking straight towards the impressive Sulitelma massif, boiling with clouds, dressed in mighty glaciers. On a clear day, few views between Grövelsjön and Treriksröset match this one.

The trail swings east around the northern shore of Pieskehaure and leads to a couple of bridges. A few kilometers of walking will take you to Pieskehaurestugan, an overnight hut with a host and a small store. You can follow a trail east from that hut that will take you on a beautiful route to Kvikkjokk and Kungsleden, should you want to switch to Lapland East, where you then connect to the route 4.5. I suggest not; much of the best on Lapland West is yet to come.

Instead, you follow the trail towards the northeast and find that you are now on one branch of Nordkalottenleden, coming from Kvikkjokk. There is another branch, coming from the town of Sulitelma in Norway. Nordkalottleden starts/ends in two places. We will get back to Nordkalottleden in several of my later route descriptions.

The trail moves up a wide, flat valley and leads to a ford of medium difficulty right by a couple of huts (closed). Directly after there is another, more difficult ford to manage at Hadditjåhkå.

This creek is said to be challenging at times. Early in the season is likely such a time, or after heavy rains. I have forded Hadditjåhkå three times without any problems, but this has always been in late July or early August when flows are generally lower.

The map shows a couple of alternative fords that might be worth looking for if fording where the trail hits the creek seems difficult. These other options are within a couple of hundred meters upstream or downstream of the trail.

After fording, you are heading up into the valley of Gaijilavagge, under the mountain of Jiegnaffo. For those botanically interested,

The semaphor at Mavasjaure.

there are endemic plants way up high on that mountain. On a clear
day, I have heard that you can see both the Atlantic to the west and
the Gulf of Bothnia to the east from the top of it.

Like in all valleys, the winds can be strong in Gaijilavagge. Many
years ago, a corner peg attachment of my friend's tent was ripped in
the night. He managed to fix it with some string and rocks but did
not enjoy running around in his underwear in the wind and rain. I
slept through it all in my tent.

Coming down from Gaijilavagge, the trail follows the creek Stad-
dajåhkå to the bridge where the branch of Nordkalottenleden from
Sulitelma joins. If you have time and energy to spare, you can take
the trail to Sårjåsjavrre and visit the perhaps most beautifully located
of all tourist huts in the Swedish mountains. The house, now called
Sårjåsjaurestugan on the map, was built almost a hundred years ago

Peskehaure with Sulitelma left of center.

by a private donor to honor her father on the condition it should be named "Konsul Perssons stuga" after him. I feel that wish should be honored, but the people in power do not seem to feel the same way.

However, most of us are eager to get to Treriksröset, and we continue past the falls, down to Staddajåkkstugan. This is an overnight hut with a host and a small store run by STF.

The trail continues north to Staloluokta, on lake Virihaure. This is a famous lake, and many famous people have named it the most beautiful in Sweden.

Staloluokta is a sizable summer camp for the Sami. You can usually buy smoked fish and homemade bread at the hostel. Staloluokta is an excellent place to resupply, there are lodgings and a well-stocked store, but you must cook for yourself. The hostel is run by Badjelannda Laponia Tourism (BLT), an organization owned by the Sami in Laponia.

Laponia is a UNESCO World Heritage and contains the three neighboring national parks of Padjelanta, Sarek, and Stora Sjöfallet. BLT manages all huts along Padjelantaleden. They are overnight huts with a host and a small store, like the STF huts. www.padjelanta.se is a good place for information on this.

From Staloluokta, you can hike in many directions. I recommend traveling through Sarek and connecting to Lapland East, described in 4.9. You can also stay on Lapland West and walk to Ritsem (4.10) or to Kvikkjokk and Lapland East (4.9).

The falls in Staddajåkk.

Virihaure with Staloluokta on the right.

4.9 Staloluokta – Sarek – Aktse or Sitojaure

Total distance: 80 or 89 km plus 12 km respectively 8 km by boat

Distances between waypoints:

⇨ Staloluokta, overnight hut

17 km

⇨ Duottar, overnight hut

12 km

⇨ Alggajavrre, lake

21 km

⇨ Skarja, bridge

5 km

⇨ Tjåggnårisjåhkå, creek

13 km

⇨ Skårkistugan, hut (closed)

21 km

⇨ Nationalparksgräns, near Nammasj

8 km, boat

⇨ Aktse, overnight hut

To Rinim on Sitojaure:

Tjåggnårisjåhkå, creek

25 km

⇨ Rinim

12 km, boat

⇨ Sitojaurestugorna, overnight huts

Effort: Medium to High. Some steep climbs, willow, and bogs

Skills: High. Off-trail navigation. Some unmarked paths that are not always easy to follow. Few huts. Several fords of medium to high difficulty.

Summary: :If there is one area you should not miss on a Green Ribbon hike, it is Sarek. Lots have been written about this magnificent area; I will not expand on that. There are many ways to cross Sarek; these are two that both connect with Kungsleden on Lapland East (4.5).

You have several, or even many, options leaving Staloluokta. One is to continue north on Padjelantaleden/Nordkalottleden to Akkastugorna and Ritsem (4.10). From Ritsem north to Kungsleden you take Ritsem – Hukejaure - Sälka (4.11)

Looking towards the Duottar huts.

Another way from Staloluokta is to walk Padjelantaleden in the other direction, taking it down beautiful Tarradalen and into Kvikkjokk. In Kvikkjokk, you connect to Kungsleden and follow that trail north (4.5).

However, the most rewarding routes out of Staloluokta will involve cross-country travel through Sarek National Park. Sarek is the wildest and most spectacular of all Swedish National Parks. I strongly advise you not to miss it on your way north. Since there are plenty of guidebooks on Sarek in different languages, I will only mention a few route options.

Leaving Staloluokta, you take Padjelantaleden east, towards Kvikkjokk, as far as the Duottar hut site. This has an overnight hut with a host and a small store. Before crossing the bridge to the huts, you leave the trail, turn left, and follow the western shore of Duottarjavrre. At the northern end of this lake, you turn east, walk south of Oarjep Rissavarre and make your way towards the lake Alggajavrre, situated at a beautiful gate into Sarek.

Alggavagge.

Before getting to that lake, you ford Alep Sarvesjåhkå at a suitable place on the flat, near the renvaktarstuga. A good rule of thumb is that those huts are usually situated close to good fords. The ford should be of medium difficulty unless you wade early in the season, during snowmelt. You should be able to find slow-moving water east of the renvaktarstuga, even if it might be deep.

After this crossing, you follow the creek north to Alggajavrre; there are some beautiful campsites on the west side, overlooking the lake and the valley towards the east. The cover photo of this book shows an example.

Willow brush is a bit of a bother as you follow the lake's southern shore. The fording of the creek coming down from the glacier on Sarvestjåhkkå should be no big problem. Since it is glacier feed, there will be less water in it after a cold night than after a hot day.

There are numerous small creeks in the delta close to the lake, but one or two are sizable. I have always forded the stream Alg-gajåhkå close to the lake, on the principle that it is easier to ford several smaller branches of a creek instead of one single channel. I used the sandbank fanning out into the lake itself for fording on one occasion.

The aim is to use the faint path shown on the map going along Alggavagge north of the valley bottom. Once you are there, you will encounter a lot of willows but no main obstacle until you reach the valley of Guohpervagge, coming from the west. You ford the Guohperjåhkå west of where Galmmejåhkå joins it and stay on elevation towards Skarja and the bridge across Smajlajåhkå. There you will also find a rest hut.

At Skarja, you are at what is sometimes called The Heart of Sarek. You are surrounded by some of the most spectacular mountain scenery in the Swedish mountains, rivaled only by the area around Kebnekaise to the north. Skarja is also a place with plenty of campsites, where hikers tend to congregate because of the bridge.

I was once offered cheese and grappa by two young Italians who had been very taken by the vast, wild areas in northern Sweden and kept coming back, winter and summer. Their Italian, alpinist friends could never understand why they walked for several days to climb a mountain lower than one you could climb in a day in Italy and be back in the village for dinner.

One option from Skarja is to go north through Ruohtesvagge and connect with Padjelantaleden coming from Staloluokta and going to Akkastugorna and Ritsem (4.10).

You are now in the upper reaches of the famed Rapadalen (Rapa Valley). I suggest you go southeast from Skarja, down Rapadalen. There is a path that divides after the ford across Tjåggnårisjåhkå. This ford has a bad reputation, particularly early in the season. The times I have waded it, the ford has been of medium difficulty. If it looks unfordable near the trail, you should follow it upstream in search of a better spot. This creek is glacier-fed, so fording in the early morning is an option, before glacier melting has come to its peak.

The path divides after the ford (WGS84 67.356444, 17.722833), and you must choose. Going right will take you down Rapadalen to Aktse, where you can take Kungsleden north on Lapland East (4.5). If you have not been to Rapadalen before, I suggest taking this route.

Going left, you can go through Basstavagge to Rinim, where you can take a boat and connect to Kungsleden at Sitojaurestugorna (4.5). I will return to that.

The right-hand path towards Rapadalen soon climbs very steeply to the "short-cut valley" Snavvavagge, which will take you to the perhaps most glorious overlook in the mountains of Sweden, that over Rapaselet. From the top, where the descent begins towards Skårkistugan (locked), you can see the delta, lakes, ponds, and river arms in intricate shapes and colors. On the opposite side of the valley, there is the soaring wall of Bielloriehppe, reaching almost a thousand meters from the valley floor. There are plenty of nice camp spots on your way down to the birch forest.

The path down Rapadalen will run through this birch forest down to the national park boundary. Along the way, several fords can be problematic early in the season. At the national park boundary, south of the solitary mountain of Nammasj, you can catch a boat that will take you to Aktse. It usually runs on a schedule, mornings and evenings. Check prices ahead and it is likely a cash business.

At Aktse, you will find a beautifully located old farmstead and a hut managed by the STF with a host and a small store. Kungsleden runs right past the front door. This is described in the chapter Kvikkjokk – Saltoluokta (4.5).

Now let us return to Tjåggnårisjåhkå and instead take the left-hand path. This will lead you to Basstavagge and Rinim and a boat across Sitojaure. Basstavagge is the opposite of the walk down lush Rapadalen towards Aktse. It is a high alpine valley with a lot more rocks than plant life. It is austere and almost forbidding, but its steep rock walls and glacier-fed streams also have their charms. You will not have encountered anything like this so far on The Green Ribbon.

Basstavagge has a couple of fords of medium to high difficulty, depending on the season and the weather. Walking upstream towards the glaciers and/or fording in the morning are helpful strategies if crossing near the valley floor looks impossible.

The view after coming out of Basstavagge and seeing the turquoise width of silt-colored Sitojaure, reflecting the sunlight, spreading towards the horizon, is something you will not easily forget.

Camp near Ribabluokta.

At the shore of the lake, you find Rinim, where a Sami family lives in summer, and you can catch a boat ride. You can either take the boat to Ribakluokta or Sitojaurestugorna. The latter is a hut site on Kungsleden, with a host and a small store. Ribaluokta is a shorter boat ride, and there is a well-marked trail to Kungsleden, north of Sitojaurestugorna. Check prices ahead and prepare for a cash-only business.

Connecting with Kungsleden in this area means hiking to Saltoluokta and then continuing on best part of Kungsleden, north from Vakkotavare to Abisko (4.6).

4.10 Staloluokta – Akka/Ritsem

Total distance: 57 km plus 11 km by boat

Distances between waypoints:

⇨ Staloluokta, overnight hut

10 km

⇨ Arasluokta, overnight hut

12 km

⇨ Låddejåhkå, overnight hut

22 km

⇨ Gisuris, overnight hut

13 km

⇨ Akkastugan, overnight hut

11 km, båt

⇨ Ritsem, mountain lodge

Effort: Low to Medium. Some climbs.
Skills: Low. Good trail, bridges, and overnight huts.

Summary: This is a lovely route with some spectacular views of the big lakes on your left and the mountains of Sarek on your right. Boat transport to Ritsem, where there is a lodge and road access with regular buses to Gällivare. From Ritsem you continue to Kungsleden between Singi and Sälka (4.11).

From Staloluokta, you follow Padjelantaleden north along Virihaure. This is also part of Nordkalottleden. Arasluokta is another Sami summer camp for a different Sami village than Staloluokta. Badjelannda Laponia Tourism (BLT) manages the huts (and all other huts in Padjelanta National Park). They are overnight huts with a host and a small store, like the STF huts. Long ago, I spent a good portion of a summer here, radio-tracking dead reindeer calves. This was done from both planes and on foot.

The trail from Arasluokta has some ups and downs, crossing the river Mellätno on a bridge before arriving at Låddejåhkå overnight hut.

After the hut, the trail climbs and curves around a mountain with lovely views of the big lake Vasstenjavrre. Hiking west of the great lakes in this area, towards the Norwegian border, is great, but difficult to access. For this reason, that area is very little visited.

There are bridges at Vuojatädno that would take you along Nordkalottleden to Vaisaluoktastugan, also with a boat connection to

Ritsem. Still, Padjelantaleden continues along the south side of the river to Kutjaure. At Vuojatstugan, there is an open hut marked on some maps. At the time of writing, this is not correct. There is no open hut at Vuojatstugan. The next open hut is at Gisuris.

You can exit or enter Sarek through Ruohtesvagge to the south and connect to the routes described in the chapter Staloluokta – Sarek – Aktse or Sitojaure (4.9).

From Gisuris and onwards, you are in birch forest. You walk beneath the beautiful mountain Akka, sometimes called The Queen of Lapland. Coming out of Ruothesvagge from Sarek some years ago I had a problematic ford across Rakkasjåhkå, south of Akka, because the rocks were covered thinly with silt from the glacier, making them extremely slippery.

However, along Padjelantaleden you will not encounter Rakkasjåhkå, but will cross the impressive rapids of Vuojatädno on a bridge, and reach Akkastugan, situated on the huge hydropower dam Akkajaure. You can determine what is a dam and what is a natural lake from the sterile stretch of shoreline usually visible, created by the frequent rise and fall of the water level in a dam.

STF manages Akkastugan, and there is a host and a small store. There is also a regular ferry across the dam to Ritsem from nearby Änonjalme. At Ritsem, there are lodgings, a café, and a store with food and some hiking gear. Compared to Saltoluokta, I find the Ritsem lodge extremely lacking in charm, just a bunch of barracks, left-overs from the hydropower construction era. There is a road and regular bus connections with Gällivare. You continue north on Nordkalottleden (4.11).

Sami storage hut (front) near Änonjalme.

4.11 Ritsem – Hukejaure – Sälka

Total distance: 62 km

Distances between waypoints:

⇨ Ritsem, mountain lodge

  21 km

⇨ Sitasjaure, overnight hut

  20 km

⇨ Hukejaure, overnight hut

  17 km

⇨ Kungsleden

  4 km

⇨ Sälka, overnight hut

Effort: Low.

Skills: Low. Roads, good trails, bridges, and overnight huts.

Summary: A lot of road walking or close-to-road walking north from Ritsem on a route heavily impacted by hydropower exploitation. You are on Nordkalottleden through an area visited by few hikers. South of Sälkastugorna, you connect to Kungsleden (4.6) and Lapland East.

The trail from Ritsem going north is Nordkalottleden, on or near a gravel supply road to the hydropower dam at Sitasjaure, where the overnight huts are. There is a host and a small store.

The trail crosses the dam and becomes more interesting as it climbs. There are a couple of bridges as you hike towards Hukejaurestugan, which is nicely situated on a small hill in the harsh tundra landscape. It is a hut seldom visited, especially compared to Kungsleden, not far to the east. There is a host and a small store.

From Hukejaure, the trail is easy to follow and curves around the low mountain Raktas. As you approach the steep-sided valley Cuhcavaggi, there is a ford, which is usually wide and easy to cross.

Walking through Cuhcavaggi, you have some impressive views of the Kebnekaise massif. It dominates the view as you enter the broad and beautiful valley of Tjäktavagge. You cross a bridge and climb until you reach Kungsleden (4.6), turning left towards Sälkastugorna.

Tjäktjavagge - view of Kungsleden between Singi and Sälka-

Sälka is a big hut-place, beautifully located with impressive peaks around. There is a host and a small store. From Sälka, there are lots of route alternatives, not only Kungsleden, almost all in spectacular surroundings. Some are mentioned in the description of route 4.6. Lapland West and Lapland East share Kungsleden to Alesjaurestugorna, where West leaves (4.12).

4.12 Alesjaure – Katterjåkk

Total distance: 47 km

Distances between waypoints:

⇨ Alesjaure, overnight hut

   15 km

⇨ Unna Allakas, overnight hut

   8 km

⇨ Valfojåkka, rest hut

   11 km

⇨ Stuor Kärpel, rest hut

   13 km

⇨ Katterjåkk, mountain lodge

Effort: Low to Medium. Some steep ascents.

Skills: Medium. Good trails, few overnight huts, some medium fords.

Summary: Leaving Kungsleden at Alesjaure on a route taking you away from routes north via Abisko. The walk along the border to Norway from Valfojåkka rest hut takes you through some remarkable, rocky, and seldom traveled terrain. In Katterjåkk, there is a store, a lodge and regular buses towards Abisko, Kiruna, and Narvik. You continue on a beautiful off-trail route to Pålnostugan (4.13). Routes 4.14 and 5.1 will also take you to Pålnostugan, on trails and roads.

The trail to the hut at Unna Allakas branches off from Kungsleden a couple of kilometers north of the Alesjaure huts. It takes you up a steep slope to a wild mountain plateau. The first time I crossed this was on skis on a lovely, sunny day late in April. The last time I walked it, on my Green Ribbon thru-hike, I had just about the worst weather experience I have ever had in the Swedish summer mountains, temperatures at 3–4 C, wind, rain, and sleet.

The trail dips steeply down to the Unna Allakas hut, with a host and a small store. This is a seldom visited hut site right on the Norwegian border. You can, if you prefer, reconnect to Kungsleden by taking the path east to Abiskojaurestugorna, but I suggest you take the trail going north, following the border to Katterjåkk. The trail climbs past the old mining operation at Sjangeli and reaches the rest hut at Valfojåkka. North of the hut, you have a couple of fords. One is on the trail, the other, more northerly, said to be easier and more of an option if the first ford is difficult.

Now you are hiking through a bare-swept rocky landscape in the valley Dossagemvaggi. It is certainly worth a visit; I find it very special. It won't be easy to find any campsites until you reach the area around the rest hut at Stuor Kärpel.

A ford might be problematic about 1 kilometer north of the Stuor Kärpel hut. In that case, an optional place to ford might be a bit downstream from the trail, at the confluence of the two creeks.

The landscape slowly becomes more benign, and as you approach Gatterjavri, you will be walking on meadows. A bridge below Katterjaurestugan (locked) will take you on a trail/road below some ski slopes and then to Katterjåkk through a tunnel beneath the railway. The railway is a significant artery of the Swedish economy, bringing endless iron ore trains from the mines in Kiruna and Gällivare to the harbor in Narvik.

In Katterjåkk, you have a mountain lodge, a restaurant, and a well-stocked store for resupplies. The lodge is managed by Friluftsfrämjandet (The Swedish Outdoor Association) and will likely hold a box for you.

From Katterjåkk, you can go to Lapland East (4.14) or West (4.13). Both will take you to Pålnostugan, where you have other route options (5.3 and 5.5). You can also walk to Abisko via 5.1 and pick up route 5.2 for boat transport to Kattuvuoma.

Marvelous rocky terrain in Dossagemvaggi.

Tents at Alisjávri.

4.13 Katterjåkk – Pålnostugan

Total distance: 30 km

Distances between waypoints:

⇨ Katterjåkk, mountain lodge

   15 km

⇨ Bajip Njuorajavri, bridge

   6 km

⇨ Njuoraluspi, bridge

   3 km

⇨ Njuoraätno, bridge

   6 km

⇨ Pålnostugan, rest hut

Effort: Low to Medium. A few climbs and some bogs. Mostly off-trail hiking.

Skills: Medium to High. A lot of off-trail navigating, some bogs. No huts.

Summary: This is an excellent wilderness route through tundra and forest, with low hills around you and lovely views to the south. Not an area where hikers move. At Pålnostugan, you can connect with Nordkalottleden, following it through Norway to Treriksröset (5.5). Or you can stay in Sweden, following the border cross-country to Vuoskojaure and then trails to Treriksröset (5.3 and 5.4).

This is another favorite that I have walked several times. It is mostly cross country through a seldom traveled area with impressive views of the mountains and the lake Torneträsk to the south.

You start out going west from Katterjåkk on a path to Riksgränsen. There you skirt the camping site down by the lake, take the trail north along Viepmatluokta and keep left, crossing Geadajohka on the bridge.

From the bridge, you aim for the path going east of the low mountain Rohccevarri. Somewhere around the knob right east of the top of that mountain you leave the trail and make your way cross-country towards the bridge at the southeast corner of lake Bajip Njuorajavri (WGS84 68.495722, 18.316389). There is a lodge, often closed, but one corner of the building is open as a rest and rescue hut.

View looking back towards Riksgränsen and Katterjåkk.

The bridge and lodge at Bajip Njuorajavri.

The bridge across Njuoraeatnu.

Pålnostugan.

The waypoints to guide you to your goal, Pålnostugan, are simply the bridges in between, that you can see on the map. From Bajip Njuorajavri, you navigate next to the Njuoraluspi bridge (WGS84 68.504861, 18.432167). You are moving along the boundary of Vadvettjåkka National Park, seldom visited because of its inaccessibility.

After the Njuoraluspi bridge, you make your way east to another bridge across Njuoraeatnu (WGS84 68.504333, 18.487722).

I advise you to stay away from the lake shores as you hike across this area since the shores are often steep and with thick vegetation. Stay reasonably high, minimize elevation changes, and do not be afraid to use the bogs for walking. Often it is easier, sometimes not. By now, if you have taken some of my suggested wild routes earlier, you probably have a feeling for how to proceed.

From the last bridge, you travel straight towards Pålnostugan, choosing your route. As you get closer to that hut, you will find meadows and other remnants of the farm it once was. Pålnostugan is a rest hut that can be used overnight but lacks a host or service. You are now on Nordkalottleden, this trail coming from Tornehamn and Abisko (5.1). You can also get to Pålnostugan from Katterjåkk using route 4.14 and 5.1.

From Pålnostugan, you can take the well-marked Nordkalottleden, with plenty of overnight huts, through Norway to Treriksröset. This is what I call The Norwegian Route (5.5). If you stay on what I call The Swedish Route, this is a wilder walk without huts, all the way to Treriksröset (5.3 and 5.4). It is a bit longer and more challenging, through an enormous expanse with few people, no service, and the feeling of a vast wilderness I have only encountered in northern Canada and Alaska.

4.14 Katterjåkk – Tornehamn

Total distance: 22 km

Distances between waypoints:

⇨ Katterjåkk, mountain lodge

   5 km

⇨ Vassijaure, railway station

   4 km

⇨ Låktatjåkka, trail fork

   13 km

⇨ Nordkalottleden, near Tornehamn, trail fork

Effort: Low.

Skills: Low.

Summary: This short route lets you connect with Nordkalottleden from Abisko and leads to Pålnostugan (5.1). An off-trail alternative from Katterjåkk to Pålnostugan is described in 4.13. From Pålnostugan, you can choose The Norwegian Route (5.5) or The Swedish Route (5.3).

From Katterjåkk, you follow Rallarleden (The Navvy Trail) east along the railway. The railway was built in the early 1900s, with this trail as a supply road. The impressive railway building at Vassijaure was built where the rails from Sweden were forged to the rails from Norway, completing the railway. The trail runs close to, and sometimes almost on, the highway E10. I you manage to block out the nearness of a highway and a railway, it is a trail with lovely views, but parts can be wet.

At the east end of lake Baktajavri, the trail merges with the highway briefly. After a road bridge across a creek, it meets Nordkalottleden (WGS84 68.440583, 18.59941). This trail comes from Abisko and goes towards Pålnostugan; the route is described in the section Abisko to Pålnostugan (5.1).

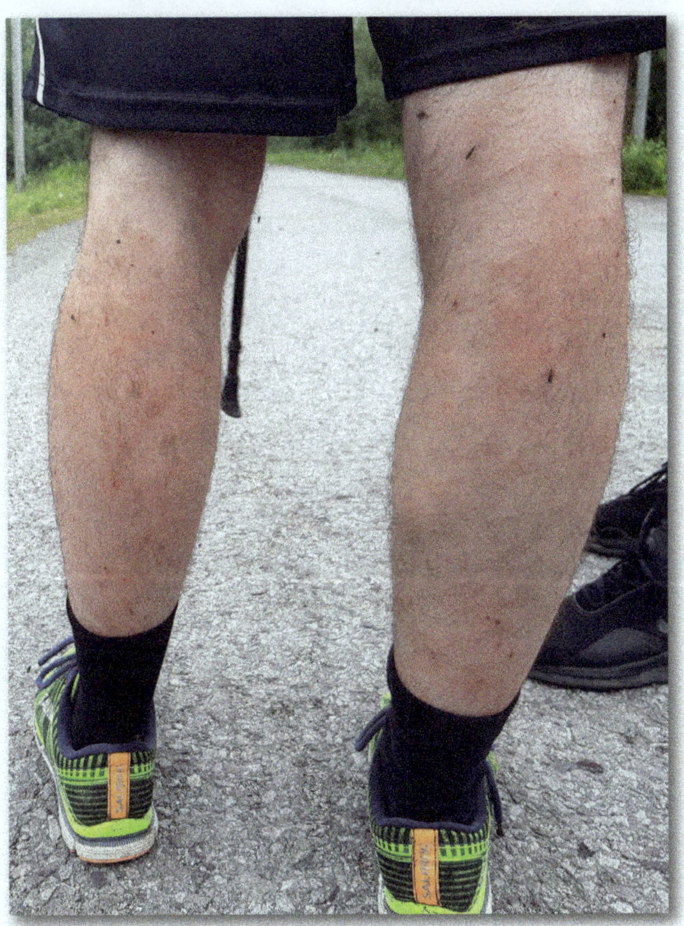

Road walking is punishing for the feet - mosquitous are punishing for the calves.

Section 5: Abisko – Treriksröset

I suggest two primary alternatives if you have arrived in Abisko by Lapland East. One I have chosen to call The Norwegian Route; it simply means that you follow the Nordkalottleden and pass Pålnostugan before entering Norway on your way to Treriksröset (5.5). The trail is well marked and serviced by cabins through Norway and re-enters Sweden slightly south of Pältsastugan.

If you have walked the wilder Lapland West and arrived in Katterjåkk, you can join Nordkalottleden in Tornehamn (4.14) and follow it to Pålnostugan. You can also hike off-trail from Katterjåkk to Pålnostugan (4.13) and then take The Norwegian Route.

The second alternative, The Swedish Route from Abisko, has two variations, to begin with. They later converge at Vuoskojaure and leads you north to Treriksröset. The first variety is taking Nordkalottleden to Pålnostugan (5.1), where you leave that trail. This route takes you off-trail through some wild and magnificent country between the Norwegian border and lake Torneträsk, to Vuoskojaure (5.3).

The second variety means leaving Abisko and walking east along the highway E10 for 50 kilometers to a place on the lake, near Torneträsk Station. If you have arranged a boat to take you across the lake Torneträsk, you then proceed past Kattuvuoma to Vuoskojaure (5.2). The off-trail route from Pålnostugan (5.3) will join there. You then follow the trail north via Kummavuopio to Treriksröset (5.4).

The Swedish and Norwegian Routes

Nordkalottleden through Norway can be strenuous and holds more spectacular mountains than The Swedish Route (which Norway always has). It is a very well-marked, well-traveled trail with plenty of luxurious huts (which Norway always has). These huts are usually locked, and you need a key. You can get this by contacting Den Norske Turistforening (DNT), the Norwegian Tourist Association.

Treriksröset
Pältsa
Kummavuopio
Hurvejåkka
Dividalen
Narvik
Pålnostugan
Katterjåkk
Tornehamn
Abisko
Vuoskojaure
Unna Allakas
Torneträsk station
Alesjaure
NORWAY
SWEDEN
Sälka
Kebnekaise 2111 m
Ritsem
Torneälven
Sarek 2089 m
Kalixälven
Saltoluokta
Sarek
Rinim
Duottar
Stora Lulevatten
Aktse
Kvikkjokk
Skalka
0
50 km
5

The Swedish Route has lots of off-trail hiking but also an almost total absence of any kind of hut, even when there is a trail. This very desolation is scarce and, at least to me, holds a great charm. I have walked both the Swedish and Norwegian routes, and neither one

will disappoint. Nordkalottleden is well documented through books and online blogs, so I will be brief on that. The Swedish alternative between Torneträsk and the Norwegian border is not well known, and more details are given.

5.1 Abisko – Tornehamn – Pålnostugan

Total distance: 20 km

Distances between waypoints:

⇨ Abisko Turist, mountain lodge

  7 km

⇨ Björkliden, mountain lodge

  4 km

⇨ Tornehamn

  2 km

⇨ Trail from Katterjåkk

  7 km

⇨ Pålnostugan, rest/overnight hut

Effort: Low.

Skills: Low.

Summary: This is a short route that follows Nordkalottleden from Abisko. Near Tornehamn, the route from Katterjåkk (4.14) joins. After Pålnostugan, you can choose between The Norwegian Route (5.5) or The Swedish Route to Vuoskojaure (5.3) and then on to Treriksröset (5.4).

To begin with, you leave Abisko on Nordkalottleden, also called Rallarleden (The Navvy Trail), and head west along the shore of Torneträsk briefly, before passing under highway E10.

Fairly soon, you will come to Björkliden, a classic mountain ski resort. There is food and lodgings available. Rallarleden was built as a supply trail when the railway was constructed. It continues towards Tornehamn and the chapel with the cemetery for some of the navvies and others who worked on the railway. It has become a bit famous for this reason, and the most famous grave is probably that of Svarta Björn (The Black Bear). She was a reputedly strong and beautiful woman who cooked for the navvies and died young. Little is known of her background.

The trail leaves highway E10, and the route from Katterjåkk (4.14) joins from the west ((WGS84 68.440583, 18.59941). Having left Rallarleden and now entirely on Nordkalottleden, rocky terrain accompanies you to a bridge across Njuoraeatnu. From then on, you are mostly in lush birch forest all the way to Pålnostugan.

Pålnostugan is a rest hut that serves as an overnight hut without a host or service. From Pålnostugan, you can follow the route along Nordkalottleden, mainly through Norway, to Treriksröset (5.5). Another option is to stay in Sweden, taking a walk off-trail in wild country to Vuoskojaure (5.3).

At Vuoskojaure, the other alternative on The Swedish Route, with boat transport across Torneträsk via Kattuvuoma, joins (5.2).

You take Nordkalottleden from Abisko.

The Swedish Route is considerably flatter and more desolate than The Norwegian Route.

5.2 Abisko – Vuoskojaure

Total distance: 63 km plus 10 km by
  boat

Distances between waypoints:

⇨ Abisko Turist, mountain lodge

  45 km

⇨ Torneträsk, boat jetty

  10 km

⇨ North shore, boat jetty

  5 km

⇨ Kattuvuoma, houses

  13 km

⇨ Vuoskojaure, bridge

Effort: Low. Lots of road walking on a big highway. Easy trail across tundra.

Skills: Low. Tent needed.

Summary: More than half of this route is hardtop road walking (E10). Local trail angels run the boat from a jetty north of Torneträsk Station, and they are not always available. At Vuoskojaure the route alternative Pålnostugan – Vuoskojaure (5.3) joins.

This is a tricky part of The Green Ribbon to describe because the boat ride depends very much on variables that can change from one week, or one year, to another. Apart from those along Kungsleden, most boat rides depend on people being in their summer houses, enjoying helping hikers, and not minding making a bit of money. All of which can change quickly. This means you probably cannot be sure of getting a boat ride across Torneträsk until you are in Abisko and can make an agreement by phone. But you can try earlier. Phone numbers can probably be had from the Green Ribbon website or their Facebook group.

Luckily you are not stuck, you always have the option of taking Nordkalottleden to the Pålnoviken hut, and there you can choose between The Norwegian or The Swedish Route, numbered 5.5 and 5.3.

If you have boat transport arranged you must walk almost to Torneträsk railway station, not to be confused with the lake itself, also called Torneträsk. Leaving Abisko, there is a path to Abisko Östra, where there is also a store and lodgings. You more or less have to walk on the highway for over 40 kilometers from then on. I can happily say that I have not done this, nor do I want to, but I have talked to people who have.

You do not walk all the way to the Torneträsk railway station; but instead, you take a left when you get close to it and follow a minor road down to the lake and a jetty. That is where the boat will pick you up. (WGS84 68.228778, 19.721722).

I have been warned by people running these boats that there is a risk that high winds on the lake will keep the boat from being able to pick you up. Torneträsk is known for waves accelerating from the western end, all along the lake, and now you are at the eastern end. You might have to wait or cancel. Cell phone coverage is not reliable.

The boat ride will take you to a bay southeast of the mountain Njalloaivi, where a road will lead to Kattuvuoma. This is a village that is more of a sparse congregation of houses.

From Kattuvuoma, you follow the trail, a wide quad trail, north to the very spread-out village of Vuoskojaure. Neither Kattuvuoma nor Vuoskojaure has any kind of commercial services.

237

Do not expect to connect from this phone booth nor from your mobile phone, in Vuoskojaure.

5.3 Pålnostugan – Vuoskojaure

Total distance: 73 km (depends)

Distances between waypoints:

⇨ Pålnostugan, rest hut/overnight hut

  17 km

⇨ Goaivojavri, lake

  22 km

⇨ Bajip Duoptejavrrit, lake

  34 km

⇨ Vuoskojaure, bridge

Effort: Medium to High. Mostly easy walking but some steep climbs, off-trail hiking, and bogs.

Skills: High. Off-trail navigating, no huts, few hikers.

Summary: This is a wild and woolly route that I genuinely recommend. You are on your own, and there are some tricky passages at the mountain Salmmecohkat. One option is to cut across the border into Norway and then back to Sweden and Vuoskojaure, where this route connects to the one from Abisko via Kattuvuoma. The total distance depends a lot on the choices you make en route.

This is a route where you must make many decisions on your own. I have not walked every possible option across this area; some alternatives I have from people who have walked them. So, take my descriptions as inspiration, not as something you should follow religiously.

From Pålnostugan, it is 1,5 kilometers to the Norwegian border, but you do not walk quite that far. There are two small lakes right before the borderline, the northernmost almost touching it. You leave the trail and head east between those two lakes and towards a steep but brief climb. There was no water to cross at the ponds when I passed, contradictory to the map. You hike in the general direction of a small lake about 500 meters straight east from the two small lakes you just left behind.

From the vicinity of that small lake, try to find the easiest route east along the border. There are many terraces, slopes, and generally

At Goaivojavri towards the southeast.

topsy-turvy terrain. You navigate this to take you to the area around the long lake just south of Lullehacorru.

You then swing northeast, in the direction of the bridge across Riksojohka and the renvaktarstuga (locked), a couple of kilometers away. The bridge is just in case; you can probably ford the creek in several places. When you have crossed the stream, you travel east on the slope, avoiding the willows, going upstream Snuvrejåhka. When the area gets reasonably flat, you cross this creek and aim for the lake Goaivojavri.

The area you are now entering is secluded, relatively flat, charming, and easy to hike—one of the highlights along this route. You follow the northern shore of Goaivojavri, then swing to the southeast, towards the lake Guollejavri. Continuing beside the creek running from that lake, you descend into a wide valley with many willows.

Avoid as many of those as you can. Now you face the most significant obstacle on this route - the mountain Salmmecohkat.

There are several ways of managing that. One is to descend south towards lake Torneträsk, go around and then hike back up the east shoulder of the mountain. On the map, that area looks both steep and riddled with willow.

The route I chose is doable but strenuous and very steep in places. I went up the creek Salmejohka and then took the branch named Salmmecahca on the map. This was completely dry in August and filled with huge blocks of stone. It was also steep. Once up, I found the descent towards the Duopptejavrrit lakes extremely step. Luckily, the slope was still covered in snow (this was the latter half of August). This snow gave good traction for my feet all the way down. Without snow, you probably must make your way south searching for less steep terrain. In steep snow like that, you also might start sliding if the snow is hard or icy.

Another option around Salmmecohkat is going north into Norway, which was not allowed when I thru-hiked. There seems to be a decent pass on the map right south of Jovnnetcohkat, from where you can make your way south and swing east north of Duoptecohkka. Then you are back on the route I walked.

From a hiker I met on the trail, I heard he had crossed Salmmecohkat along the creek south of Salmmecahca, called Balggesgorsajohka. His route is probably what I would use another time. However, Balggesgorsajohka is also steep and rocky, coming from the west. I have understood that it would help to approach it from the northwest, from the Salmmejohka direction, and hike diagonally up the slope. Make your way to the small lake on top of the pass as best as you can. From this pass, going down towards Bajip Duoptejavrrit is less steep than the snow slope I came down, slightly to the north.

The easiest way to avoid the mountain Salmmecohkat is to cross into Norway and walk most of the distance there, following the big lakes Geavdnjajavri and Leinavatn east, into Sweden to Vuoskojaure.

If you choose to cross the mountain Salmmecohkat, this crossing will most likely be the most demanding on the entire Green Ribbon. I would not necessarily consider it dangerous in decent weather, but it takes care and is slow, heavy going. If the weather is poor, it might be risky and ruin your schedule due to delay. So, packing an extra day's food is not bad for this area. It is a great experience in nice weather, which I had, with stunning views of Torneträsk and the mountains around.

When you have crossed Salmmecohkat and come to the Dupptejavrrit lakes, a good route leads straight east through the valley north of Duoptecohkka. From there, it is downhill, but be sure to stay on the north side of the deep and steep ravine of Beaivvegorsa. You then aim for the border and the renvaktarstuga southeast of Cearrovaras. As you get closer to this hut (locked), the country becomes extraordinarily rocky and broken up, dotted with small lakes. Tricky walking and I blessed my hiking poles.

Once you are in the vicinity of this hut, a good option might be to cut across the corner of Norway on the northern slopes of Gaivarri. You can then connect with the trail coming from Jorbacohkka in the south and leading to Vuoskojaure. Quad tracks leading into Norway might be used.

I did not go into Norway but was enticed by the paths from the renvaktarstuga in a southeasterly direction. They started as quad tracks, but I soon lost them; the similarity between the paths shown on the map and the terrain and the quad tracks seemed entirely incidental in that area. Thanks to the GPS, I did not lose my direction and soon stopped bothering using the tracks. Instead, I made my way off-trail as best I could.

I also had difficulties finding the trail going north from Laimoluokta but finally managed to find it south of Jorbacohka. I then followed it north to Vuoskojaure, where the route from Kattuvuoma joins (5.2).

5.4 Vuoskojaure – Kummavuopio – Treriksröset

Total distance: 99 km
Distances between waypoints:
⇨ Vuoskojaure, bridge
  15 km
⇨ Kamasjaure, rest hut
  35 km
⇨ Rostojavri, bridge
  16 km
⇨ Hurvejåkka, rest hut
  10 km
⇨ Kummavuopio, farm
  21 km
⇨ Golddaluokta, jetty
  3 km
⇨ Treriksröset (Three Country Cairn

Effort: Low to Medium. No ascents worth mentioning.
Skills: Medium to High. The trail is sometimes obscure. No overnight huts, few rest huts, few hikers.

Summary: This is a vast, rolling country with huge distances, unlike anything found in the mountains further south. Very few hikers visit; I recommend it as an experience – very different from Nordkalottleden through Norway. The trail is usually, but not always, easy to follow. After reaching Treriksröset, a boat can take you to Kilpisjärvi and Finland. Or you can hike to Kilpisjärvi, where there is service and buses.

You are in the northernmost part of Sweden. Overnight huts are almost non-existent, Pältsastugan being the only one. Though this route suggestion will not take you past that hut, it is on Nordkalott-leden (5.5). There are only a couple of rest huts between Vuoskojaure and Treriksröset.

The village of Vuoskojaure is very scattered. This is a big country, and nobody wants to crowd their neighbors. Most of the houses I saw seemed empty. Along the trail through this scattering, a rusty telephone booth is a remnant from the good old days. Or maybe just from the old days.

After Vuoskojaure, the well-marked trail towards Kamasjaure climbs to the tundra. It will be a while before you see something that can be called a forest again.

From the rest hut at Kamasjaure, you have another 50 kilometers to the next one, at Hurvejåkka. The country you move through could be described as rolling, the trail moving between and sometimes over low mountains that more like hills. It is a beautiful but lonely area. You are truly walking on the wild side here. Not much land between you and the North Pole. Not much to stop the wind or the rain either.

On the other hand, it is easy hiking and beautiful views in nice weather. But you are on your own. I have hiked this area several times, often cross country, and have no recollection of ever meeting or seeing anyone. Indeed, on my thru-hike, I met nobody from Vuoskojaure until Kummavuopio, where I waved at a guy on a quad.

At the bridge across Giehpanjohka, the well-marked trail ended. It took me an hour to pick it up, east of Sinot Sinnukkavaara; the GPS is handy in featureless terrain like this.

243

The sandhills around Ravskkasjohka.

Crossing the peaceful Kummaeno.

The trail follows an exciting array of gravel ridges along Omatjavri, with lovely views of the lakes. Should you need it, or want to, there is a fishing camp at the eastern end of the lake Rostojavri, called Råstojaure Vildmarkscamp. It is a couple of kilometers off-trail and served by helicopter. They might agree to transport and hold a box for a fee. Depending on vacancies or not, there might be lodgings and meals to be had.

The tundra keeps rolling north, and you roll along with it, past the rest hut at Hurvejåkka. The trail then enters the beautiful sandhills and valleys along Ravskkasjohka. You encounter some trees, which will accompany you past Kummavuopio, until the last tundra mountain before Treriksröset.

Along Ravskkasjohka, a trail marked on the map as Renskötarled goes west towards Pältsatugan. However, it does not lead all the way to that hut, and you have a ford and some cross-country travel to do before reaching Pältsa. I considered it as a possible route to Treriksröset but saw no advantage since it is not shorter than going via Kummavuopio. If you take The Norwegian Route, you will come to Pältsastugan and from there to Treriksröset (5.5).

At the goal!

Kummavuopio is not much of a village, only a farm with a couple of houses, close to the big Könkämä river that constitutes the border to Finland. This river can only be crossed in a few places, Keinovuopio to the south being one. That is a bigger village than Kummavuopio.

After crossing the peaceful tributary Kummaeno at Kummavuopio, you take the road west up along that river. Do not make the mistake I made and try to take a shortcut to the trail going north from Nilsivaara. Go to the beginning of the path and follow it over your last tundra incline before Treriksröset.

The views overlooking lake Kilpisjärvi are great as you descend to Golddaluokta, where there is a boat service across the lake to the village of Kilpisjärvi and Finland. You might use this on your way back from Treriksröset.

There are only another three kilometers of walking on a small road before you reach Treriksröset. You might meet some day-trippers who has come by boat to visit Treriksröset. There are some fences and somewhat complicated paths, but you will find the big, yellow concrete blob on Golddajavri that you have been striving for. Congratulations, you made it!

5.5 Pålnostugan – Nordkalottleden – Treriksröset

Total distance: 147 km

Distances between waypoints:

⇨ Pålnostugan, rest/overnight hut

  3 km

⇨ Lappjordhytta, overnight hut

  24 km

⇨ Altevasshytta, overnight hut

  12 km

⇨ Gaskashytta, overnight hut

  18 km

⇨ Vuomahytta, overnight hut

  19 km

⇨ Dividalshytta, overnight hut

  24 km

⇨ Daertahytta, overnight hut

  16 km

⇨ Rostahytta, overnight hut

  18 km

⇨ Pältsastugan, overnight hut

  13 km

⇨ Treriksröset (Three Country Cairn)

Effort: Medium to High. Several steep climbs.

Skills: Low to Medium. Well-marked trail with plenty of huts and hikers but exposed terrain in bad weather.

Summary: You are on Nordkalottleden all the way to Treriksröset. This is a beautiful hike through beautiful mountains. Its prominent peaks and nice huts are almost the opposite of the comparatively flat Swedish Route. Comfortable that way, but more demanding physically due to the steeper terrain.

From Pålnostugan, it is 1,5 kilometers to Norway, where you pass right by one of the cairns that stud the border in places. It is steep going to the nice hut Lappjordhytta. Unless you have managed to pay and secure a key through DNT (Den Norske Turistforening (The Norwegian Tourist Association), it will be locked unless lodgers are in the hut. You can count on this for all the DNT huts along Nordkalottleden. Check at the DNT website.

A ladder covered with planks serves as a bridge near Gaskashytta.

247

The trail continues steeply uphill for a while, after which it is easy going on a well-marked path. In my experience, albeit limited, trails are better maintained in Norway than in Sweden, maybe thanks to DNT.

You pass a Sami summer camp along the route and encounter lots of mud churned by quad bikes in that valley. Descending, the trail becomes a road. You reach Altvasshytte, overlooking the long hydropower dam of Altavatnet. There were massive protests by occupants against the building of this dam during the 1970s; the Norwegian government even considered calling on the army to support. Fortunately, this was stopped at the last minute.

There is a road at Altavatnet and a nearby village, Innset. The road continues towards Gaskashytta for a bit, after which there is a ford and confusion of quad tracks. After passing Gaskashytta, you climb and follow the long valley towards Vuomahytta; about halfway, you encounter a lot of rocks.

After Vuomahytta, you enter the beautiful Anjavass valley, descending into the birch forest where you continue to the famous

One of the canyons near Anjavasshytta.

248

national park of Dividalen, passing an exciting system of canyons as you descend.

The trail up to Dividalshytta is steep, first through a lovely forest and then, after the hut, a continued climb to the tundra. The passage to the hut Daertahytta is all above the tree line and was clouded, cold, and wet when I hiked it. In good weather, it is probably magnificent.

After Daertahytta, the trail climbs very steeply. Halfway up, in the rain, I met and talked to a German woman in ultralight rain gear who seemed to know everything about lightweight equipment. The cold and rain made it easy to end the conversation before revealing my shortcomings. As fate would have it, I met this woman again the following summer on a Coast2Coast Sweden hike I had organized. It took us a while to recognize each other without rain jacket hoods that only had our noses visible.

The rest of the trail towards Rostahytta is exposed until it descends a couple of kilometers steeply before that hut and comes to a bridge. After the hut, the trail climbs gently onto a gigantic, dry moor with easy walking but little water. This moor takes you to the

The trail crosses into Sweden near Mount Pältsa.

Swedish border, and soon you can see the distinctive peak Pältsan to the north. This is almost the only mountain that is more than a mound in this very northernmost part of Sweden. The prominent peaks are all on the Norwegian side.

Pältsastugan is an overnight hut managed by STF, with a host and a small store (late in the season, there might not be much to buy). It might be possible to have them hold a box for you, but it will probably cost; most everything is flown in since there is no road access.

From Pältsa, the long, distant goal of Treriksröset is no longer so distant. What you have been aiming for since Grövelsjön is at hand. The trail climbs some mounds before crossing a flat expanse. You take the left-hand trail towards Treriksröset and skip Golddaluokta for now. Later, you might catch a boat there, taking you to Finland and civilization.

The trail descends into the birch forest, and there are some fences and somewhat complicated paths, but you will find the big, yellow concrete blob on Golddajavri that you have been striving for. Congratulations, you made it!

Books and other sources

English

📖 Fenton, Danielle and Wayne: *Kungsleden: All you need to know to complete Sweden's Royal Trail*

📖 Grundsten, Claes: *Kungsleden: The Royal Trail Through Arctic Sweden*

📖 Karlson, Bosse and Bjelvenstedt, Bosse: *Sarek: Mountain Tours 1970–2016*

📖 Laing, Mike: *Trekking the Kungsleden: The King's Trail through Northern Sweden*

📖 Neregård, Fredrik: *Best hiking in Sweden: Kungsleden*

German

📖 Bickel, Peter: *Nordskandinavien – Der Wanderführer: Nordkalottleden, Kungsleden, Padjelantaleden.*

📖 Drexel, Rebecca and Hell, Benjamin: *Schweden: Sarek (Der Weg is das Ziel)*

📖 Grundsten, Claes: *Wanderführer Sarek – Trekking in Schweden*

📖 Henneman, Michael: *Skandinavien: Nordkalottleden*

📖 Henneman, Michael: *Schweden: Padjelantaleden*

📖 Heyne, Klaus: *Trekking im Sarek*

Swedish

📖 Berggren, Annika: *Kungsleden – vandringsturer och utflykter*

📖 Fowelin, Hans: *Vandringsturer i Sarek*

📖 Grundsten, Claes: *På Fjälltur: Kungsleden*

📖 Grundsten, Claes: *På Fjälltur: Sarek*

📖 Neregård, Fredrik och Hedman, Sam: *Fjällvandra längs Kungsleden Abisko – Hemavan*

📖 Neregård, Fredrik: *Fjällvandra längs Nordkalottleden*

📖 Neregård, Fredrik: *Fjällvandra i Sarek*

📖 Piehl, Karl-Johan: *Sarek: vandring, löpning och klättring med lättviktspackning*

On a packrafting trip with Mt Kebnekaise on the horizon.

Late fall camp in the far north, along Lainio river.

One of the best views in the Swedish mountains, from the top of Skierfe, looking down on Lake Lajtavrre.

www.ingramcontent.com/pod-product-compliance
Lightning Source LLC
Chambersburg PA
CBHW040135160726
48006CB00014B/1503